CECIL COUNTY
PUBLIC LIBRARY
301 Newark Ave.
Elkton, MD 21921

NOV

10935206

Careers in Focus

JOURNALISM

Careers in Focus

JOURNALISM

Ferguson
An imprint of ☑️ Facts On File

Careers in Focus: Journalism

Copyright © 2006 by Facts On File, Inc.

All rights reserved. No part of this book may be reproduced or utilized in any form or by any means, electronic or mechanical, including photocopying, recording, or by any information storage or retrieval systems, without permission in writing from the publisher. For information contact

Ferguson
An imprint of Facts On File, Inc.
132 West 31st Street
New York NY 10001

Library of Congress Cataloging-in-Publication Data
Careers in focus. Journalism.
    p. cm.
    Includes index.
    ISBN 0-8160-5843-1 (hard. : alk. paper)
    1. Journalism—Juvenile literature. 2. Journalism—Vocational guidance—
Juvenile literature. I. J.G. Ferguson Publishing Company.
    PN4776.C35 2005
    070.4'023—dc22   2005013374

Ferguson books are available at special discounts when purchased in bulk quantities for businesses, associations, institutions, or sales promotions. Please call our Special Sales Department in New York at (212) 967-8800 or (800) 322-8755.

You can find Ferguson on the World Wide Web at http://www.fergpubco.com

Text design by David Strelecky

Printed in the United States of America

MP JT 10 9 8 7 6 5 4 3 2 1

This book is printed on acid-free paper.

Table of Contents

Introduction

Careers in Focus: Journalism describes a variety of careers in the deadline-driven, yet rewarding, world of journalism—at newspapers, magazines, publishing companies, and radio and television stations. These careers are as diverse in nature as they are in their earnings and educational requirements. Earnings range from minimum wage or less for entry-level desktop publishing specialists and cartoonists to $1 million for top network news anchors. A few of these careers—such as editorial and research assistants—require a few years of post-secondary education, but are excellent starting points for a career in the industry. Other technically oriented jobs, such as printing press operators and assistants, require a high school diploma and on-the-job training. Many positions in this industry (such as art directors, editors, writers, and journalism teachers) require a minimum of a bachelor's degree.

The outlook for journalism jobs is expected to be keenly competitive in the coming years. In fact, the *Career Guide to Industries* predicts that employment in the newspaper, magazine, and book publishing industries will decline by 1 percent through 2012. Employment in journalistic broadcasting is expected to increase by 9 percent through 2012—slower than the 16 percent growth expected for all industries.

Despite these predictions, the journalistic publishing and broadcast industries play a major role in our lives. They are responsible for providing timely and sometimes urgent information to the public. Also, more and more print and broadcast entities are producing online versions, which will require editors, writers, desktop publishing specialists, and artists with skills specific to Web page development. Opportunities will be especially strong for workers who have advanced education and knowledge of the latest technology.

Some of the articles in *Careers in Focus: Journalism* appear in Ferguson's *Encyclopedia of Careers and Vocational Guidance,* but have been updated and revised with the latest information from the U.S. Department of Labor, professional organizations, and other sources. In addition, the following articles have been written specifically for this book: Copy Editors, Editorial and Research Assistants, Fashion Writers and Editors, Food Writers and Editors, Journalism Teachers, and News Anchors.

Each article contains a number of sections that provide a comprehensive overview of the career. The **Quick Facts** section provides a brief summary of the career, including recommended school subjects, personal skills, work environment, minimum educational requirements, salary ranges, certification or licensing requirements, and employment outlook. This section also provides acronyms and identification numbers for the following government classification indexes: the *Dictionary of Occupational Titles* (DOT), the *Guide for Occupational Exploration* (GOE), the National Occupational Classification (NOC) Index, and the Occupational Information Network (O*NET)-Standard Occupational Classification System (SOC) index. The DOT, GOE, and O*NET-SOC indexes have been created by the U.S. government; the NOC index is Canada's career-classification system. Readers can use the identification numbers listed in the Quick Facts section to access further information about a career. Print editions of the DOT (*Dictionary of Occupational Titles.* Indianapolis, Ind.: JIST Works, 1991) and GOE (*The Complete Guide for Occupational Exploration.* 3d ed. Indianapolis, Ind.: JIST Works, 2001) are available at libraries. Electronic versions of the NOC (http://www23.hrdc-drhc.gc.ca) and O*NET-SOC (http://online.onetcenter.org) are available on the World Wide Web. When no DOT, GOE, NOC, or O*NET-SOC numbers are present, this means that the U.S. Department of Labor or Human Resources Development Canada have not created a numerical designation for this career. In this instance, you will see the acronym "N/A," or not available.

The **Overview** section is a brief introductory description of the duties and responsibilities involved in this career. Oftentimes, a career may have a variety of job titles. When this is the case, alternative career titles are presented.

The **History** section describes the history of the particular job as it relates to the overall development of its industry or field.

The **Job** describes the primary and secondary duties of the job.

Requirements discusses high school and postsecondary education and training requirements, any certification or licensing that is necessary, and other personal requirements for success in the job.

Exploring offers suggestions on how to gain experience in or knowledge of the particular job before making a firm educational and financial commitment. The focus is on what can be done while still in high school (or in the early years of college) to gain a better understanding of the job.

The **Employers** section gives an overview of typical places of employment for the job.

Starting Out discusses the best ways to land that first job, be it through the college placement office, newspaper ads, or personal contact.

The **Advancement** section describes what kind of career path to expect from the job and how to get there.

Earnings lists salary ranges and describes the typical fringe benefits.

The **Work Environment** section describes the typical surroundings and conditions of employment—whether indoors or outdoors, noisy or quiet, social or independent. Also discussed are typical hours worked, any seasonal fluctuations, and the stresses and strains of the job.

The **Outlook** section summarizes the job in terms of the general economy and industry projections. For the most part, Outlook information is obtained from the U.S. Bureau of Labor Statistics and is supplemented by information taken from professional associations. Job growth terms follow those used in the *Occupational Outlook Handbook*. Growth described as "much faster than the average" means an increase of 36 percent or more. Growth described as "faster than the average" means an increase of 21 to 35 percent. Growth described as "about as fast as the average" means an increase of 10 to 20 percent. Growth described as "more slowly than the average" means an increase of 3 to 9 percent. Growth described as "little or no change" means an increase of 0 to 2 percent. "Decline" means a decrease of 1 percent or more.

Each article ends with **For More Information,** which lists organizations that provide information on training, education, internships, scholarships, and job placement.

Careers in Focus: Journalism also includes photos, informative sidebars, and interviews with professionals in the field.

Whether you are interested in art, current events, fashion, photography, or politics, there is a chance for you to have a rewarding career in the field of journalism. Read about the different opportunities available, and be sure to contact the organizations listed for more information.

Art Directors

QUICK FACTS

School Subjects
Art
Computer science
Journalism

Personal Skills
Artistic
Communication/ideas

Work Environment
Primarily indoors
Primarily one location

Minimum Education Level
Bachelor's degree

Salary Range
$34,160 to $69,050 to
$114,390+

Certification or Licensing
None available

Outlook
About as fast as the average

DOT
164

GOE
01.01.01

NOC
5131

O*NET-SOC
27-1011.00

OVERVIEW

In journalistic publishing, *art directors* work with artists, photographers, illustrators, desktop publishing specialists, and text and photo editors to develop visual images and generate copy. They are responsible for evaluating existing illustrations and photographs, choosing new illustrations and photographs, determining presentation styles and techniques, hiring both staff and freelance talent, working with layouts, and preparing budgets.

Art directors are also employed by advertising agencies to oversee the creation of an advertisement or ad campaign, television commercials, posters, and packaging, as well as in film and video and on the Internet.

In sum, art directors are charged with informing and educating consumers. They supervise both in-house and off-site staff, handle executive issues, and oversee the entire artistic production process. There are more than 147,000 artists and art directors working in the United States.

HISTORY

The first art directors were probably staff illustrators for book publishers. As the publishing industry grew more complex and incorporated new technologies such as photography and film, art direction evolved into a more supervisory position and became a full-time job. Publishers and advertisers began to need specialists who could acquire and use illustrations and photos. Women's magazines such as *Vogue* (http://www.style.com/vogue) and *Harper's Bazaar* (http://www.harpersbazaar.com), and photo magazines, such as *National Geographic* (http://www.nationalgeographic.com), relied so much on illustration and photography that the photo editor and art director began to carry as much power as the text editor.

Today's art directors supervise almost every type of visual project produced. Through a variety of methods and media, from magazines and newspapers to film and television, comic books, and the Internet, art directors communicate ideas by selecting and supervising every element that goes into the finished product.

THE JOB

Art directors are responsible for all visual aspects of printed or on-screen projects. Art directors, even those with specialized backgrounds, must be skilled in and knowledgeable about design, illustration, photography, computers, research, and writing in order to supervise the work of graphic artists, photographers, illustrators, desktop publishing specialists, text and photo editors, and other employees.

In publishing, art directors may begin with the editorial department's concept or develop one in collaboration with these and other publishing professionals. Once the concept is established, art directors need to decide on the most effective way to communicate it by asking a variety of questions. What is the overall tone of the publication? (Serious? Thought-provoking? Comedic?) How will the illustrations complement the text? If only a small amount of text is being used, how will the illustrations be used to communicate information to the reader? What type of format (print or online or both) will be used? Additionally, if an article or feature is being revised, existing illustrations must be reevaluated.

After deciding what needs to be illustrated, art directors must find sources that can create or provide the art. Photo agencies, for example, have photographs and illustrations on thousands of different subjects. If, however, the desired illustration does not exist, it may have to be commissioned or designed by one of the staff designers or illustrators. Commissioning artwork means that the art director contacts a photographer or illustrator and explains what is needed. A price is negotiated, and the artist creates the image specifically for the art director.

Once the illustrations and other art elements have been secured, they must be presented in an appealing manner. The art director supervises (and may help in the production of) the layout of the piece and presents the final version to the editorial director. Laying out is the process of figuring out where every image, headline, and block of text will be placed on the page. The size, style, and method of reproduction must all be specifically indicated so that the image is recreated as the director intended it.

Technology has been playing an increasingly important role in the art director's job. Most art directors, for example, use a variety of computer software programs, including Adobe InDesign, FrameMaker, Illustrator, Photoshop, QuarkXPress, and CorelDRAW. Many others create and oversee websites for publishers and work with other interactive media and materials, including CD-ROM, touch-screens, multidimensional visuals, and new animation programs.

Art directors usually work on more than one project at a time and must be able to keep numerous, unrelated details straight. They often work under pressure of a deadline and yet must remain calm and pleasant when dealing with staff and managers. Because they are supervisors, art directors are often called upon to resolve problems, not only with projects but with employees as well.

Art directors are not entry-level workers. They usually have years of experience working at lower-level jobs in the field before gaining the knowledge needed to supervise projects. Art directors in the publishing industry have to know how printing presses operate and how content is created and laid out for online publications. They should also be familiar with a variety of production techniques in order to understand the wide range of ways that images can be manipulated to meet the needs of a project.

REQUIREMENTS

High School

A college degree is usually a requirement for art directors; however, in some instances, it is not absolutely necessary. A variety of high school courses will give you both a taste of college-level offerings and an idea of the skills necessary for art directors on the job. These courses include art, drawing, art history, graphic design, illustration, photography, advertising, and desktop publishing.

Math courses are also important. Most of the elements of sizing an image involve calculating percentage reduction or enlargement of the original picture. This must be done with a great degree of accuracy if the overall design is going to work. For example, type size may have to be figured within a thirty-second of an inch for a print project. Errors can be extremely costly and may make a publication look sloppy.

Other useful courses that you should take in high school include journalism, business, computing, English, and technical drawing.

Postsecondary Training

According to the American Institute of Graphic Arts, nine out of 10 artists have a college degree. Among them, six out of 10 have majored in graphic design, and two out of 10 have majored in fine arts. In addition, almost two out of 10 have a master's degree. Along with general two- and four-year colleges and universities, a number of professional art schools offer two-, three-, or four-year programs with such classes as figure drawing, painting, graphic design, and other art courses, as well as classes in art history, writing, business administration, communications, and foreign languages.

Courses in journalism, advertising, marketing, photography, layout, desktop publishing, and fashion are also important for those interested in becoming art directors. Specialized courses, sometimes offered only at professional art schools, may be particularly helpful for students who want to go into art direction. These include typography, animation, storyboard, website design, and portfolio development.

Because of the rapidly increasing use of computers in design work, it is essential to have a thorough understanding of how computer art and layout programs work. At smaller publishers, the art director may be responsible for operating this equipment; at larger publishers, a staff person, under the direction of the art director, may use these programs. In either case, the director must know what can be done with the available equipment.

In addition to course work at the college level, many universities and professional art schools offer graduates or students in their final year a variety of workshop projects, desktop publishing training opportunities, and internships. These programs provide students with opportunities to develop their personal design styles as well as their portfolios.

Other Requirements

The work of an art director requires creativity, imagination, curiosity, and a sense of adventure. Art directors must be able to work with all sorts of specialized equipment and computer software, such as graphic design programs, as well as make presentations on the ideas behind their work.

The ability to work well with different people is a must for art directors. They must always be up-to-date on new techniques, trends, and attitudes. And because deadlines are a constant part of the work, an ability to handle stress and pressure well is key.

Accuracy and attention to detail are important parts of the job. When art is done neatly and correctly, the public usually pays no notice. But when a publication is done poorly or sloppily, people will notice, even if they have had no design training. Other requirements for art directors include time-management skills and an interest in media and people's motivations and lifestyles.

EXPLORING

High school students can get an idea of what an art director does by working on the staff of the school newspaper, magazine, or yearbook. It may also be possible to secure a part-time job assisting the advertising director of the local newspaper or to work at an advertising agency. Developing your own artistic talent is important, and this can be accomplished through self-training (reading books and practicing) or through courses in painting, drawing, or other creative arts. At the very least, you should develop your "creative eye," that is, your ability to develop ideas visually. One way to do this is by familiarizing yourself with great works, such as paintings or highly creative newspaper and magazine layouts, websites, advertisements, motion pictures, videos, or commercials.

Students can also become members of a variety of art or advertising clubs around the nation. Check out the website of Paleta: The Art Project (http://www.paletaworld.org) to join a free art club. In addition to keeping members up-to-date on industry trends, such clubs offer job information, resources, and a variety of other benefits.

EMPLOYERS

More than 147,000 artists and art directors are employed in the United States. Art directors are employed at newspaper, magazine, and book publishers throughout the United States. While publishers of all sizes employ art directors, smaller publishers often combine the positions of graphic designer, illustrator, photo editor, and art director. And although opportunities for art direction can be found all across the nation and abroad, many larger publishing companies in such cities as Chicago, New York, and Los Angeles usually have more openings and higher pay scales than smaller publishing companies.

In addition to opportunities in publishing, art directors are employed by advertising agencies, museums, packaging firms, photography studios, marketing and public relations firms, desktop publishing outfits, digital pre-press houses, printing companies, film production houses, multimedia developers, computer game developers, and television stations.

STARTING OUT

Since an art director's job requires a great deal of experience, it is usually not considered an entry-level position. Typically, a person on a career track toward art director is hired as an assistant to an established director. Recent graduates wishing to enter the field should have a portfolio of their work containing seven to 10 samples to demonstrate their understanding of the type of publication (newspapers, magazines, or books) and the media (print or online) in which they want to work.

Serving as an intern is a good way to get experience and develop skills. Graduates should also consider taking an entry-level job in an art department at a newspaper or magazine to gain initial experience. Either way, aspiring art directors must be willing to acquire their credentials by working on various projects. This may mean working in a variety of areas, such as advertising, marketing, editing, and design.

College publications offer students a chance to gain experience and develop portfolios. In addition, many students are able to do freelance work while still in school, allowing them to make important industry contacts and gain on-the-job experience at the same time.

ADVANCEMENT

Many people who get to the position of art director do not advance beyond the title but move on to work at more prestigious newspapers and magazines. Competition for positions at well-known newspapers and magazines continues to be keen because of the sheer number of talented people interested. At smaller publications, the competition may be less intense, since candidates are competing primarily against others in the local market.

EARNINGS

According to the U.S. Department of Labor, a beginning art director or an art director working at a small newspaper or magazine can expect to make $34,160 or less per year in 2003, with experienced art directors working at larger newspapers or magazines earning

$114,390 or more. Mean annual earnings for art directors employed by newspaper, magazine, book, and directory publishers were $69,050 in 2003. The median annual earnings for art directors working in all industries were $62,260. Again, it is important to note that these positions are not entry level; beginning art directors have probably already accumulated several years of experience in the field for which they were paid far less.

Most publishing companies employing art directors offer insurance benefits, a retirement plan, and other incentives and bonuses.

WORK ENVIRONMENT

Art directors usually work in studios or office buildings. While their work areas are ordinarily comfortable, well lit, and ventilated, they often handle glue, paint, ink, and other materials that may pose safety hazards, and they should, therefore, exercise caution.

Art directors at publishing companies usually work a standard 40-hour week. Many, however, work overtime during busy periods in order to meet deadlines.

While art directors work independently while reviewing artwork and reading copy, much of their time is spent collaborating with and supervising a team of employees, often consisting of editors, photographers, illustrators, graphic artists, and desktop publishing specialists.

OUTLOOK

The extent to which art director positions are in demand, like many other positions, depends on the economy in general; when times are tough, people and media companies spend less, and cutbacks are made. When the economy is healthy, employment prospects for art directors will be favorable. The U.S. Department of Labor predicts that employment for art directors will grow about as fast as the average for all other occupations through 2012. Publishers always want some type of illustration to enhance their newspapers, magazines, books, and websites. People who can quickly and creatively generate new concepts and ideas will be in high demand.

However, it is important to note that the supply of aspiring art directors is expected to exceed the number of job openings. As a result, those wishing to enter the field will encounter strong competition for salaried, staff positions as well as for freelance work. And although the Internet is expected to provide many opportunities for artists and art directors, some publishing companies are hiring employees without formal art or design training to operate computer-aided design systems and oversee work.

FOR MORE INFORMATION

For more information on design professionals, contact
American Institute of Graphic Arts
164 Fifth Avenue
New York, NY 10010
Tel: 212-807-1990
http://www.aiga.org

The Art Directors Club is an international, nonprofit organization of directors in advertising, graphic design, interactive media, broadcast design, typography, packaging, environmental design, photography, illustration, and related disciplines. For information, contact
Art Directors Club
106 West 29th Street
New York, NY 10001
Tel: 212-643-1440
Email: info@adcglobal.org
http://www.adcglobal.org

For information on the graphic arts, contact
Graphic Artists Guild
90 John Street, Suite 403
New York, NY 10038-3202
Tel: 212-791-3400
http://www.gag.org

For industry statistics, information on diversity, and to view a PowerPoint presentation entitled "Tips on Finding a Job in Magazines" visit the MPA website.
Magazine Publishers of America (MPA)
810 Seventh Avenue, 24th Floor
New York, NY 10019
Tel: 212-872-3700
Email: mpa@magazine.org
http://www.magazine.org

Visit this NASAD website for information on schools.
  National Association of Schools of Art and Design (NASAD)
  11250 Roger Bacon Drive, Suite 21
  Reston, VA 20190-5248
  Tel: 703-437-0700
  Email: info@arts-accredit.org
  http://nasad.arts-accredit.org

For information on careers in newspapers and industry facts and figures, contact
  Newspaper Association of America
  1921 Gallows Road, Suite 600
  Vienna, VA 22182-3900
  Tel: 703-902-1600
  Email: IRC@naa.org
  http://www.naa.org

For information on design issues in newspapers and other news publications, contact
  Society for News Design
  1130 Ten Rod Road, Suite F-104
  North Kingstown, RI 02852-4177
  Tel: 401-294-5233
  http://www.snd.org

Cartoonists

OVERVIEW

Cartoonists are illustrators who draw pictures and cartoons to amuse, educate, and persuade people. They work for newspapers, magazines, cartoon syndicates, book publishers, and advertising agencies.

HISTORY

Broadly speaking, cartoons and other types of illustration have been used to educate and entertain people since the dawn of time. But it wasn't until the invention of movable metal type by Johannes Gutenberg in about 1450 that cartoons and other illustrations began to reach large audiences. The Protestant Reformer Martin Luther created illustrated pamphlets to convey his ideas about reforming the Roman Catholic Church and distributed them to peasants, most of whom were illiterate. As people realized the power of images in educating the public and influencing their opinions, cartoons and other illustrations began to appear in printed publications throughout Europe.

In the United States, Benjamin Franklin's "Join, or Die" is considered the first political cartoon. Its depiction of a snake severed into eight segments was created to encourage the colonies to cooperate in dealing with the Iroquois Nation at the Albany Congress of 1754. By the Civil War, political cartoons had become increasingly important as a means of conveying opinions and information to the American public. Thomas Nast's pro-Union cartoons were so effective that President Abraham Lincoln called him the North's "best recruiting sergeant." Nast is best known, though, for his satirical cartoons in *Harper's Weekly* from 1869 to 1872 that spotlighted the

QUICK FACTS

School Subjects
Art
Computer science
Journalism

Personal Skills
Artistic
Communication/ideas

Work Environment
Primarily indoors
Primarily one location

Minimum Education Level
High school diploma

Salary Range
$10,400 to $55,840 to $78,000

Certification or Licensing
None available

Outlook
About as fast as the average

DOT
141

GOE
01.04.01

NOC
5241

O*NET-SOC
27-1013.03

abuses of power by William "Marcy" Tweed and his Tammany Hall political machine in New York City. When Tweed tried to elude justice by fleeing to Spain, it is said that authorities used Nast's cartoons to help identify Tweed.

In 1894, the continuity strip, which featured a comedic or dramatic story that continued from issue to issue, was invented as a means to boost newspaper circulation. By the late 1890s, newspaper magnates Joseph Pulitzer and William Randolph Hearst were using color comics as supplements in their Sunday papers to increase readership. In 1904, *A. Piker Clerk,* by Clare Briggs, became the first daily comic strip, and was soon followed by many other dailies. In 1912, William Randolph Hearst created the first syndication agency, which sold reprint rights for articles and comic strips to other newspapers in the United States and abroad. Today, this groundbreaking agency is known as the King Features Syndicate.

As cartoons grew in popularity, cartoonists realized that they needed organizations to represent their professional interests. In 1946, the National Cartoonists Society was founded. Today, it boasts a membership of 600 of the world's top cartoonists who specialize in creating editorial cartoons, humorous magazine and book illustrations, sports cartoons, comic strips, comic books, comic panels, animation, gag cartoons, greeting cards, and advertising. The Association of American Editorial Cartoonists (AAEC) was founded in 1957 to promote interest in editorial cartooning and represent the professional interests of editorial cartoonists. The AAEC has approximately 200 members.

THE JOB

Cartoonists draw illustrations for newspapers, magazines, books, greeting cards, and other publications. Cartoons most often are associated with newspaper comics or with editorial commentary, but they are also used to highlight and interpret information in publications as well as in advertising.

Whatever their individual specialty, cartoonists translate ideas onto paper in order to communicate these ideas to an audience. Sometimes the ideas are original; at other times they are directly related to the news of the day or to the content of a magazine article. After cartoonists come up with ideas, they discuss them with their employers, who include editors, art directors, or news directors. Next, cartoonists sketch drawings and submit these for approval. Employers may suggest changes, which the cartoonists then make. Cartoonists use a variety of art materials, including pens, pencils, markers, crayons, paints, transparent washes, and shading sheets. They may draw on paper, acetate, or bristol board.

Editorial cartoonists comment on society by drawing pictures with messages that are funny or thoughtful. They often use satire to illuminate the failings or foibles of public figures. Their drawings often depict political or social issues, as well as events in the worlds of sports and entertainment. *Portraitists* are cartoonists who specialize in drawing caricatures. Caricatures are pictures that exaggerate someone's prominent features, such as a large nose, to make them recognizable to the public. Most editorial cartoonists are also talented portraitists.

Comic strip artists tell jokes or short stories in newspapers and magazines with a series of pictures. Each picture is called a frame or a panel, and each frame usually includes words as well as drawings. *Comic book artists* also tell stories with their drawings, but their stories are longer, and they are not necessarily meant to be funny.

REQUIREMENTS

High School

If you are interested in becoming a cartoonist, you should study art in high school in addition to following a well-rounded course of study. To comment insightfully on contemporary life, it is useful to study political science, history, and social studies. English and communications classes will also help you to become a better communicator.

Postsecondary Training

Cartoonists need not have a college degree, but employers usually expect some art training. Typical college majors for those who attend college include art, communications, English, or liberal arts. Training in computers in addition to art can be especially valuable. If you are interested in becoming an editorial cartoonist, you should take courses in journalism, history, and political science.

Other Requirements

Cartoonists must be creative. In addition to having artistic talent, they must generate ideas, although it is not unusual for cartoonists to collaborate with writers for ideas. They must be able to come up with concepts and images to which the public will respond. They must have a good sense of humor and an observant eye to detect people's distinguishing characteristics and society's interesting attributes or incongruities.

EXPLORING

If you are interested in becoming a cartoonist, you should submit your drawings to your school paper. You also might want to draw posters to publicize activities, such as sporting events, dances, and meetings.

Student membership in professional associations is another good way to learn more about this career. The Association of American Editorial Cartoonists offers student membership to college students who create editorial cartoons on a regular basis for a college newspaper.

Scholarship assistance for art students is available from some sources. For example, the Society of Illustrators awards some 125 scholarships annually to student artists from any field. Students do not apply directly; rather, they are selected and given application materials by their instructors.

EMPLOYERS

Employers of cartoonists include newspapers, magazines, book publishers, cartoon syndicates, and advertising agencies. In addition, a number of these artists are self-employed, working on a freelance basis.

STARTING OUT

Formal entry-level positions for cartoonists are rare, but there are several ways for artists to enter the cartooning field. Most cartoonists begin by working piecemeal, selling cartoons to small publications, such as community newspapers, that buy freelance cartoons. Others assemble a portfolio of their best work and apply to publishers or the art departments of advertising agencies. In order to become established, cartoonists should be willing to work for what equals less than minimum wage.

ADVANCEMENT

Cartoonists' success, like that of other artists, depends on how much the public likes their work. Very successful cartoonists work for prestigious newspapers and magazines at the best wages; some become well known to the public.

EARNINGS

Freelance cartoonists may earn anywhere from $100 to $1,200 or more per drawing, but top dollar generally goes only for big, full-

Major Newspaper Syndicates

As you develop your artistic abilities, you might decide to submit your work to a syndicate. A syndicate is a company that edits, promotes, and distributes editorial cartoons, comic strips, illustrations, and text-based articles to newspapers in the United States and throughout the world. In short, a syndicate will take your cartoon or other artistic creation and help it reach (for a percentage of your earnings, of course) many more readers than you would ever reach on your own. If you think you are ready for the big time, contact one of the major syndicates listed below for information on submission guidelines.

Cartoonists and Writers Syndicate
67 Riverside Drive,
Suite 1D
New York, NY 10024
http://www.cartoonweb.com/
aboutcws

Creator's Syndicate
5777 West Century Boulevard,
Suite 700
Los Angeles, CA 90045
http://www.creators.com/
index2_submissions.html

King Features Syndicate
888 Seventh Avenue, 2nd Floor
New York, NY 10019
http://www.kingfeatures.com/
subg.htm

Los Angeles Times Syndicate
218 South Spring Street
Los Angeles, CA 90012
http://www.tmsinternational.
com

Tribune Media Services
435 North Michigan Avenue,
Suite 1400
Chicago, IL 60611
http://www.tms.tribune.com

United Media
(United Feature Syndicate/
   Newspaper Enterprise
   Association)
200 Madison Avenue, 4th Floor
New York, NY 10016
http://www.unitedfeatures.com/
ufsapp

Universal Press Syndicate
4520 Main Street, Suite 700
Kansas City, MO 64111-7701
http://www.amuniversal.com/up/
index.htm

Washington Post Writers Group
1150 15th Street, NW
Washington, DC 20071-9200
http://www.postwritersgroup.com/
writersgroup.htm

color projects such as magazine cover illustrations. Most cartoonists average from $200 to $1,500 a week ($10,400 to $78,000 per year), although syndicated cartoonists on commission can earn much more.

Salaries depend on the work performed. Although the U.S. Department of Labor does not give specific information regarding cartoonists' earnings, it does note that the median earnings for salaried fine artists who worked for newspaper and book publishers were $55,840 in 2003. Salaried cartoonists, who are related workers, may have earnings similar to this figure.

Self-employed cartoonists do not receive fringe benefits such as paid vacations, sick leave, health insurance, or pension benefits. Those who are salaried employees of companies, agencies, newspapers, magazines, and the like do typically receive these fringe benefits.

WORK ENVIRONMENT

Most cartoonists work in big cities where employers such as magazine and newspaper publishers are located. They generally work in comfortable environments, at drafting tables or drawing boards with good light. Staff cartoonists work a regular 40-hour workweek but may occasionally be expected to work evenings and weekends to meet deadlines. Freelance cartoonists have erratic schedules, and the number of hours they work may depend on how much money they want to earn or how much work they can find. They often work evenings and weekends but are not required to be at work during regular office hours.

Cartoonists can be frustrated by employers who curtail their creativity, asking them to follow instructions that are contrary to what they would most like to do. Many freelance cartoonists spend a lot of time working alone at home, but cartoonists have more opportunities to interact with other people than do most working artists.

OUTLOOK

Employment for artists and related workers is expected to grow about as fast as the average through 2012, according to the U.S. Department of Labor. Because so many creative and talented people are drawn to this field, however, competition for jobs will be strong.

More than half of all visual artists are self-employed, but freelance work can be hard to come by, and many freelancers earn little until they acquire experience and establish a good reputation. Competition for work will be keen; those with an undergraduate or advanced degree in art will be in demand. Experience in action drawing and computers are a must.

FOR MORE INFORMATION

For information on editorial cartooning, contact
Association of American Editorial Cartoonists
1221 Stoneferry Lane
Raleigh, NC 27606
Tel: 919-859-5516
http://info.detnews.com/aaec

For education and career information, contact
National Cartoonists Society
1133 West Morse Boulevard, Suite 201
Winter Park, FL 32789
Tel: 407-647-8839
Email: crosegal@crowsegal.com
http://www.reuben.org

*For scholarship information for qualified students in art school, have
your instructor contact*
Society of Illustrators
Museum of American Illustration
128 East 63rd Street
New York, NY 10021-7303
Tel: 212-838-2560
Email: info@societyillustrators.org
http://www.societyillustrators.org

To view a variety of editorial cartoons, visit
Daryl Cagle's Professional Cartoonists Index
http://www.cagle.com

Columnists

QUICK FACTS

School Subjects
Computer science
English
Journalism

Personal Skills
Communication/ideas
Helping/teaching

Work Environment
Indoors and outdoors
Primarily multiple locations

Minimum Education Level
Bachelor's degree

Salary Range
$17,900 to $31,240 to
$71,520+

Certification or Licensing
None available

Outlook
More slowly than the average

DOT
131

GOE
01.03.01

NOC
5123

O*NET-SOC
27-3020.00, 27-3022.00

OVERVIEW

Columnists write opinion pieces for publication in newspapers or magazines. Some columnists work for syndicates, which are organizations that sell articles to many media at once.

Columnists can be generalists who write about whatever strikes them on any topic. Most columnists focus on a specialty, such as government, politics, local issues, health, humor, sports, gossip, or other themes.

Most newspapers employ local columnists or run columns from syndicates. Some syndicated columnists work out of their homes or private offices.

HISTORY

Because the earliest American newspapers were political vehicles, much of their news stories brimmed with commentary and opinion. This practice continued up until the Civil War. Horace Greeley, a popular editor who had regularly espoused partisanship in his *New York Tribune*, was the first to give editorial opinion its own page separate from the news.

As newspapers grew into instruments of mass communication, their editors sought balance and fairness on the editorial pages and began publishing a number of columns with varying viewpoints.

Famous Washington, D.C.-based columnist Jack Anderson was known for bringing an investigative slant to the editorial page. Art Buchwald and Molly Ivins are well known for their satirical look at government and politicians. George Will and Fareed Zakaria are known for their keen analysis and opinions about government and world events.

The growth of news and commentary on the Internet has only added to the power of columnists as their thoughts, ideas, and opinions are read by millions or even billions throughout the world.

THE JOB

Columnists often take news stories and enhance the facts with personal opinions and panache. Columnists may also write from their personal experiences. Either way, a column usually has a punchy start, a pithy middle, and a strong, sometimes poignant, ending.

Columnists are responsible for writing columns on a regular basis on accord with a schedule, depending on the frequency of publication. They may write a column daily, weekly, quarterly, or monthly. Like other journalists, they face pressure to meet a deadline.

Most columnists are free to select their own story ideas. The need to constantly come up with new and interesting ideas may be one of the hardest parts of the job, but also one of the most rewarding. Columnists search through newspapers, magazines, and the Internet, watch television, and listen to the radio. The various types of media suggest ideas and keep the writer aware of current events and social issues.

Next, they do research, delving into a topic much like an investigative reporter would, so that they can back up their arguments with facts.

Finally, they write, usually on a computer. After a column is written, at least one editor goes over it to check for clarity and correct mistakes. Then the cycle begins again. Often a columnist will write a few relatively timeless pieces to keep for use as backups in a pinch, in case a new idea can't be found or falls through.

Most columnists work in newsrooms or magazine offices, although some, especially those who are syndicated but not affiliated with a particular newspaper, work out of their homes or private offices. Many well-known syndicated columnists work out of Washington, D.C.

Newspapers often run small pictures of columnists, called head shots, next to their columns. This, and a consistent placement of a column in a particular spot in the paper, usually gives a columnist greater recognition than a reporter or editor.

REQUIREMENTS

High School

You'll need a broad-based education to do this job well, so take a college prep curriculum in high school. Concentrate on English and

George Will, a political columnist, provides commentary at a baseball game, which is his favorite sport and a frequent nonpolitical topic of his columns. *(David H. Wells/Corbis)*

journalism classes that will help you develop research and writing skills. Keep your computer skills up-to-date with computer science courses. History, psychology, science, and math should round out your education. If you interested in a specific topic such as sports, politics, or developments in medicine, you should take classes that will help you develop your knowledge in that area. In the future, you'll be able to draw on this knowledge when you write your column.

Postsecondary Training

As is the case for other journalists, at least a bachelor's degree in journalism is usually required, although some journalists graduate with degrees in political science or English. Experience may be gained by writing for the college or university newspaper and through a summer internship at a newspaper or other publication. It also may be helpful to submit freelance opinion columns to local or national publications. The more published articles, called "clips," you can show to prospective employers, the better.

Other Requirements

Being a columnist requires similar characteristics to those required for being a reporter: curiosity, a genuine interest in people, the ability to write clearly and succinctly, and the strength to thrive under deadline pressure. But as a columnist, you will also require a certain wit and wisdom, the compunction to express strong opinions, and the ability to take apart an issue and debate it.

EXPLORING

A good way to explore this career is to work for your school newspaper and perhaps write your own column. Participation in debate clubs will help you form opinions and express them clearly. Read your city's newspaper regularly and take a look at national papers as well as magazines. Which columnists, on the local and national level, interest you? Why do you feel their columns are well done? Try to incorporate these good qualities into your own writing. Contact your local newspaper and ask for a tour of the facilities. This will give you a sense of what the office atmosphere is like and what technologies are used there. Ask to speak with one of the paper's regular columnists about his or her job. He or she may be able to provide you with valuable insights. Visit the Dow Jones Newspaper Fund website (http://djnewspaperfund.dowjones.com/fund) for information on careers, summer programs, internships, and more. Try getting a part-time or summer job at the newspaper, even if it's just answering phones and doing data entry. In this way you'll be able to test out how well you like working in such an atmosphere.

EMPLOYERS

Newspapers of all kinds run columns, as do certain magazines and even public radio stations, where a tape is played over the airways of the author reading the column. Some columnists are self-employed, preferring to market their work to syndicates instead of working for a single newspaper or magazine.

STARTING OUT

Most columnists start out as reporters. Experienced reporters are the ones most likely to become columnists. Occasionally, however, a relatively new reporter may suggest a weekly column if the beat being covered (for example, politics) warrants it.

Another route is to start out by freelancing, sending columns out to a multitude of newspapers and magazines in the hopes that someone will pick them up. Also, columns can be marketed to syndicates. A list of these, and magazines that may also be interested in columns, is provided in the *Writer's Market* (http://www.writersmarket.com).

ADVANCEMENT

Newspaper columnists can advance in national exposure by having their work syndicated. They also may try to get a collection of their columns published in book form. Moving from a small newspaper or magazine to a large national publication is another way to advance.

Columnists also may choose to work in other editorial positions, such as editor, editorial writer or page editor, or foreign correspondent.

EARNINGS

Like reporters' salaries, the incomes of columnists vary greatly according to experience, newspaper size and location, and whether the columnist is under a union contract. But generally, columnists earn higher salaries than reporters.

The U.S. Department of Labor classifies columnists with news analysts, reporters, and correspondents, and reports that the median annual income for these professionals was $31,240 in 2003. Ten percent of those in this group earned less than $17,900, and 10 percent made more than $71,520 annually. According to the *Annual Survey of Journalism & Mass Communication Graduates,* directed by the University of Georgia, the median salary for those who graduated in 2002 with bachelor's degrees in journalism or mass communication was $26,000. Median earnings varied somewhat by employer; for example, those working for weekly papers earned $22,000, while those working for consumer magazines earned $27,350. Although these salary figures are for all journalists (not just columnists), they provide a general range for those working in this field. However, popular columnists at large papers earn considerably higher salaries.

Freelancers may get paid by the column. Syndicates pay columnists 40 percent to 60 percent of the sales income generated by their columns or a flat fee if only one column is being sold.

Freelancers must provide their own benefits. Columnists working on staff at newspapers and magazines receive typical benefits such as health insurance, paid vacation days, sick days, and retirement plans.

WORK ENVIRONMENT

Columnists work mostly indoors in newspaper or magazine offices, although they may occasionally conduct interviews or do research on location out of the office. Some columnists may work as much as 48 to 52 hours a week. Some columnists do the majority of their writing at home or in a private office and come to the newsroom primarily for meetings and to have their work approved or changed by editors. The atmosphere in a newsroom is generally fast paced and loud, so columnists must be able to concentrate and meet deadlines in this type of environment.

OUTLOOK

The U.S. Department of Labor predicts that employment growth for news analysts, reporters, and correspondents (including columnists) will be slower than the average through 2012. Growth will be hindered by such factors as mergers and closures of newspapers, decreasing circulation, and lower profits from advertising revenue. Online publications may be a source for new jobs. Competition for newspaper and magazine positions is very competitive, and competition for the position of columnist is even stiffer because these are prestigious jobs that are limited in number. Smaller daily and weekly newspapers may be easier places to find employment than major metropolitan newspapers, and movement up the ladder to columnist will also likely be quicker. Pay, however, is less than at bigger papers. Journalism and mass communication graduates will have the best opportunities, and writers will be needed to replace those who leave the field for other work or retire.

FOR MORE INFORMATION

For a list of accredited programs in journalism and mass communications, visit the ACEJMC website.

   **Accrediting Council on Education in Journalism and Mass
      Communications (ACEJMC)**
   University of Kansas School of Journalism and Mass
   Communications
   Stauffer-Flint Hall, 1435 Jayhawk Boulevard
   Lawrence, KS 66045-7575
   http://www.ku.edu/~acejmc/STUDENT/PROGLIST.SHTML

For information on careers in nonfiction writing, education, and financial aid opportunities, contact

   American Society of Journalists and Authors
   1501 Broadway, Suite 302
   New York, NY 10036
   Tel: 212-997-0947
   http://www.asja.org

This association provides general educational information on all areas of journalism, including newspapers, magazines, television, and radio.

Association for Education in Journalism and Mass Communication
234 Outlet Pointe Boulevard
Columbia, SC 29210-5667
Tel: 803-798-0271
Email: aejmc@aejmc.org
http://www.aejmc.org

For information on jobs, scholarships, internships, college programs, and other resources, contact

National Association of Broadcasters
1771 N Street, NW
Washington, DC 20036
Tel: 202-429-5300
Email: nab@nab.org
http://www.nab.org

The SPJ has student chapters all over the United States and offers information on scholarships and internships.

Society of Professional Journalists (SPJ)
3909 North Meridian Street
Indianapolis, IN 46208
Tel: 317-927-8000
Email: questions@spj.org
http://www.spj.org

Visit the following website for comprehensive information on journalism careers, summer programs, and college journalism programs.

High School Journalism
http://www.highschooljournalism.org

INTERVIEW

Mark Brown is a columnist for the Chicago Sun-Times. *He discussed his career with the editors of* Careers in Focus: Journalism.

Q. How long have you worked in journalism?
A. I have been getting paid to write for newspapers since I was 14 years old. I am now 49. I got my first full-time newspaper job in 1978. I became a columnist four years ago.

Q. What was your college major and did it prepare you for a career as a columnist?

A. I was a journalism major. I feel that some of my college coursework was helpful—media law and a class on the philosophical framework of journalism—but I learned the practical side of the business more from working at the student paper in college.

Q. How/where did you get your first job in this field?

A. Before my freshman year in high school, I answered an ad in the local weekly paper for a sports stringer. I kept that job throughout high school, and it helped me get a similar job for a daily paper when I went to college. I later enrolled in a master's degree program with a newspaper internship component. All that experience helped me get my first real job with the *Quad-City Times*.

Q. What are your favorite topics to write about?

A. Political corruption, helping the little guy, humor. Nothing beats a column that combines all three.

Q. What are the basic components of a good column?

A. A good column holds the reader's interest from start to finish and ideally engages them to think.

Q. What are the most important qualities for columnists?

A. A columnist has to have something to say. A columnist should have some knowledge—or the ability to educate himself or herself in a hurry.

Q. What are some of the pros and cons of being a columnist?

A. Pros: Opportunity to have an impact, allowed to have an opinion, pays better, more freedom.

Cons: Relentless pressure to produce, coming up with ideas

Q. What advice would you give high school students who are interested in becoming columnists?

A. Learn the business of reporting and writing first. Experiment with an occasional opinion piece to try to find your voice. Try to do some magazine stories to experiment with writing with a point of view.

Copy Editors

QUICK FACTS

School Subjects
English
Journalism

Personal Interests
Communication/ideas
Helping/teaching

Work Environment
Primarily indoors
Primarily one location

Minimum Education Level
Bachelor's degree

Salary Range
$24,590 to $41,460 to
$77,430+

Certification or Licensing
None available

Outlook
About as fast as the average

DOT
132

GOE
01.02.01

NOC
5122

O*NET-SOC
27-3041.00

OVERVIEW

Copy editors, sometimes called *line editors*, read manuscripts for correct grammatical usage and spelling. They edit the manuscripts to conform with the publisher's style, which includes such points as capitalization, abbreviations, and the use of numbers. They polish the writing style, make sure the style and structure is consistent throughout the manuscript, and flag the text with questions about details that may need elaboration or clarification from the writer. Copy editors are employed by magazine and book publishers, newspapers, newsletters, corporations of all kinds, advertising agencies, radio stations, television stations, and Internet sites. There are approximately 130,000 editors (including copy editors) employed in the United States.

HISTORY

The history of book editing is tied closely to the history of the book and bookmaking and the history of the printing process. The 15th-century invention of the printing press by German goldsmith Johannes Gutenberg and the introduction of movable type in the West revolutionized the craft of bookmaking. Books could now be mass-produced. It also became more feasible to make changes to copy before a book was put into production. Printing had been invented hundreds of years earlier in Asia, but books did not proliferate there as quickly as they did in the West, which saw millions of copies in print by 1500.

In the early days of publishing, authors worked directly with the printer, and the printer was often the publisher and seller of the author's work. Eventually, however, booksellers began to work directly with the authors and eventually took over the role of publisher. The publisher then became the middleman between author and printer.

The publisher worked closely with the author and sometimes acted as the editor. The word *editor,* in fact, derives from the Latin word *edere* or *editum* and means "supervising or directing the preparation of text." Eventually, specialists were hired to perform the editing function. These editors, who were also called advisers or literary advisers in the 19th century, became an integral part of the publishing business.

The editor, also called the *sponsor* in some houses, sought out the best authors, worked with them, and became their advocate in the publishing house. Some editors became so important that their very presence in a publishing house could determine the quality of author that might be published there. Some author-editor collaborations have become legendary. The field has grown through the 20th and 21st century, with computers greatly speeding up the process by which copy editors and other editorial professionals move copy to the printer.

In 1997, the American Copy Editors Society was formed to represent the professional interests of copy editors. It has approximately 800 members.

THE JOB

Copy editors read manuscripts carefully to make sure that they are sufficiently well written, factually correct (sometimes this job is done by a *researcher* or *fact checker*), grammatically correct, and appropriate in tone and style for its intended readers. If a manuscript is not well written, it is not likely to be well received by readers. If it is not factually correct, it will not be taken seriously by those who spot its errors. If it is not grammatically correct, it will not be understood. If it is not appropriate for its audience, it will be utterly useless. Any errors or problems in a printed piece reflect badly not only on the author but also on the publishing house.

Copy editors use proofreaders' marks to indicate they have found a problem with the manuscript. These marks are universally understood throughout the publishing industry and help editorial professionals quickly communicate potential problems contained in a manuscript.

The copy editor must be an expert in the English language, have a keen eye for detail, and know how to identify problems. The editor will simply correct some kinds of errors, but in some cases—especially when the piece deals with specialized material—the editor may need to ask, or query, the author about certain points. An editor must never change something that he or she does not understand, since one of the worst errors an editor can make is to change something that is correct to something that is incorrect.

After a copy editor finishes editing a manuscript, it is usually reviewed by a senior copy editor and may be (but is not always) returned to the author for review. Once all parties agree that the manuscript is in its final form, it is prepared for production.

Copy editors in newspaper or magazine publishing may also be required to write headlines for articles and stories. They may make suggestions on how a story or its corresponding illustrations should appear on the page. Copy editors in book publishing are usually required to edit entire manuscripts, including the table of contents, foreword, main text, glossary, bibliography, and index. They may also proofread galleys, proofs, and advertising and marketing materials for errors.

REQUIREMENTS

High School

Copy editors must be expert communicators, so you should excel in English. You must learn to write extremely well, since you will be correcting and even rewriting the work of others. If elective classes in writing are available in your school, take them. Study journalism and take communications courses. Work as a writer or editor for the school paper. Take a photography class. Since virtually all editors use computers, take computer courses. You absolutely must learn to type. If you cannot type accurately and rapidly, you will be at an extreme disadvantage. Don't forget, however, that a successful copy editor must have a wide range of knowledge. The more you know about many areas, the more likely you will be to do well as an editor. Don't hesitate to explore areas that you find interesting. Do everything you can to satisfy your intellectual curiosity. As far as most editors are concerned, there is no useless information.

Postsecondary Training

A copy editor must have a bachelor's degree, and advanced degrees are highly recommended for editors who are interested in moving up in the industry. Most copy editors have degrees in English or journalism, but it is not unheard of for editors to major in one of the other liberal arts. If you know that you want to specialize in a field such as scientific editing, you may wish to major in the area of science of your choice while minoring in English, writing, or journalism. There are

A copy editor reviews a manuscript in her office. *(Sarah Hadley)*

many opportunities for editors in technical fields, since most of those who go into editing are interested primarily in the liberal arts. Many colleges offer courses in book editing, magazine design, general editing, and writing. Some colleges, such as the University of Chicago and Stanford University, offer programs in publishing, and many magazines and newspapers offer internships to students. Take advantage of these opportunities. It is extremely important that you gain some practical experience while you are in school. Work on the school paper or find a part-time job with a newspaper or magazine. Don't hesitate to work for a publication in a noneditorial position. The more you know about the publishing business, the better off you will be.

Other Requirements

Good copy editors are fanatics for the written word. Their passion for good writing comes close to the point of obsession. They are analytical people who know how to think clearly and communicate what they are thinking. They read widely. They not only recognize good English when they see it but also know what makes it good. If they read something they don't understand, they analyze it until they do understand it. If they see a word they don't

CECIL COUNTY
PUBLIC LIBRARY
301 Newark Ave.
Elkton, MD 21921

know, they look it up. When they are curious about something, they take action and research the subject. They are not satisfied with not knowing things.

You must be detail oriented to succeed as a copy editor. You must also be patient, since you may have to spend hours combing manuscripts for inconsistencies and style issues. If you are the kind of person who can't sit still, you probably will not succeed as a copy editor. To be a good copy editor, you must be a self-starter who is not afraid to make decisions. You must be good not only at identifying problems but also at solving them, so you must be creative. If you are both creative and a perfectionist when it comes to language, copyediting may be the line of work for you.

EXPLORING

One of the best ways to explore the field of editing is to work on a school newspaper or other publication. The experience you gain will definitely be helpful, even if your duties are not strictly editorial. Being involved in writing, reporting, typesetting, proofreading, printing, or any other task will help you to understand editing and how it relates to the entire field of publishing.

If you cannot work for the school paper, try to land a part-time job with a local newspaper or newsletter. If that doesn't work, you might want to publish your own newsletter. There is nothing like trying to put together a small publication to make you understand how publishing works. You may try combining another interest with your interest in editing. For example, if you are interested in environmental issues, you might want to start a newsletter that deals with environmental problems and solutions in your community.

Another useful project is keeping a journal. In fact, any writing project will be helpful, since editing and writing are inextricably linked. Write something every day. Try to rework your writing until it is as good as you can make it. Try different kinds of writing, such as letters to the editor, short stories, poetry, essays, comedic prose, and plays.

The American Copy Editors Society offers a wide variety of resources for aspiring and professional copy editors at its website (http://www.copydesk.org). These include articles about copyediting, a discussion board, a practice copyediting test, and suggested books and websites. The society also offers student membership to high school students who are taking journalism courses or working on a school or alternative publication.

EMPLOYERS

One of the best things about the field of editing is that there are many kinds of opportunities for copy editors. The most obvious employers for copy editors are newspapers, magazines, and books. There are many varieties of all three of these types of publishers. There are small and large publishers, general and specialized publishers, local and national publishers. If you have a strong interest in a particular field, you will undoubtedly find various publishers that specialize in it.

Another excellent source of employment is business. Almost all businesses of any size need writers and copy editors on a full-time or part-time basis. Corporations often publish newsletters for their employees or produce publications that talk about how they do business. Large companies produce annual reports that must be written and copyedited. In addition, advertising is a major source of work for copy editors, proofreaders, and writers. Advertising agencies use copy editors, proofreaders, and quality-control people, as do typesetting and printing companies (in many cases, proofreaders edit as well as proofread). Keep in mind that somebody has to work on all the printed material you see every day, from books and magazines to menus and matchbooks.

STARTING OUT

There is tremendous competition for editorial jobs, so it is important for a beginner who wishes to break into the business to be as well prepared as possible. College students who have gained experience as interns, have worked for publications during the summers, or have attended special programs in publishing will be at an advantage. In addition, applicants for any editorial position must be extremely careful when preparing cover letters and resumes. Even a single error in spelling or usage will disqualify an applicant. Applicants for editorial or proofreading positions must also expect to take and pass tests that are designed to determine their language skills.

Many copy editors enter the field as editorial assistants or proofreaders. Some editorial assistants perform only clerical tasks, whereas others may also proofread or perform basic editorial tasks. Typically, an editorial assistant who performs well will be given the opportunity to take on more and more editorial duties as time passes. Proofreaders have the advantage of being able to look at the work of editors, so they can learn while they do their own work.

The American Copy Editors Society offers job listings at its website, http://www.copydesk.org. Other good sources of information about job openings are school placement offices, classified ads in newspapers and trade journals, specialized publications such as *Publishers Weekly* (http://publishersweekly.com), and Internet sites. One way to proceed is to identify local publishers through the Yellow Pages. Many publishers have websites that list job openings, and large publishers often have telephone job lines that serve the same purpose.

ADVANCEMENT

After gaining skill and experience, copy editors may be given a wider range of duties while retaining the same title. The may advance to the position of *senior copy editor*, which involves overseeing the work of junior copy editors, or *project editor*. The project editor performs a wide variety of tasks, including copyediting, coordinating the work of in-house and freelance copy editors, and managing the schedule of a particular project. From this position, an editor may move up to become an *assistant editor,* then *managing editor,* then *editor in chief.*

At newspapers, a common advancement route is for copy editors to be promoted to a particular department, where they may move up the ranks to management positions. An editor who has achieved success in a department may become a *city editor,* who is responsible for news, or a managing editor, who runs the entire editorial operation of a newspaper.

Magazine copy editors advance in much the same way that copy editors in book publishing do. They work their way up to become senior editors, managing editors, copy chiefs, and editors in chief. In many cases, magazine copy editors advance by moving from a position on one magazine to the same position with a larger or more prestigious magazine. Such moves often bring significant increases in both pay and status.

EARNINGS

Median annual earnings for all editors were $41,460 in 2003, according to the U.S. Department of Labor. The lowest 10 percent earned less than $24,590 and the highest 10 percent earned $77,430 or more. In 2003, the mean annual earnings for all editors in newspaper and book publishing were $47,260, while those employed in radio and television broadcasting earned $41,680.

Copy editors typically receive fringe benefits such as paid vacations, sick leave, health insurance, and pension benefits. Copy editors who work on a freelance basis do not receive these benefits.

WORK ENVIRONMENT

For the most part, publishers of all kinds realize that a quiet atmosphere is conducive to work that requires tremendous concentration. It takes an unusual ability to focus to copyedit in a noisy place. Most copy editors work in private offices or cubicles.

Deadlines are an important issue for copy editors. Newspaper and magazine copy editors often have the most pressing deadlines since these publications may be produced daily or weekly. Copy editors who are employed by publications that have a presence on the Web, especially newspapers, may have to meet countless deadlines during a single day to ensure that readers have the most up-to-date information. Copy editors who are employed by book publishers have more relaxed deadlines since book publishing occurs over the course of months, not days or weeks.

OUTLOOK

According to the *Occupational Outlook Handbook*, employment of all editors will increase about as fast as the average through 2012. Competition for those jobs will remain intense, since so many people want to enter the field. Book publishing will remain particularly competitive, since many people still view the field in a romantic light. Much of the expansion in publishing is expected to occur in small newspapers and in broadcast media. In these organizations, pay is low even by the standards of the publishing business.

There will be increasing job opportunities for copy editors in Internet publishing as online publishing and services continue to grow. Advertising and public relations will also provide employment opportunities. A fairly large number of positions—both full time and freelance—become available when experienced copy editors leave the business for other fields.

FOR MORE INFORMATION

The following organization's website is an excellent source of information about careers in copyediting. The ACES organizes educational seminars and maintains lists of internships.

American Copy Editors Society (ACES)
3 Healy Street
Huntington, NY 11743
http://www.copydesk.org

The ASNE helps editors maintain the highest standards of quality, improve their craft, and better serve their communities. It preserves and promotes core journalistic values. Visit its website to read online publications such as Why Choose Journalism? *and* Preparing for a Career in Newspapers.

American Society of Newspaper Editors (ASNE)
11690B Sunrise Valley Drive
Reston, VA 20191-1409
Tel: 703-453-1122
Email: asne@asne.org
http://www.asne.org

Founded in 1958 by the Wall Street Journal *to improve the quality of journalism education, this organization offers internships, scholarships, and literature for college students. To read* The Journalist's Road to Success: A Career Guide, *which lists schools offering degrees in news-editing, and financial aid to those interested in print journalism, visit the DJNF website.*

Dow Jones Newspaper Fund (DJNF)
PO Box 300
Princeton, NJ 08543-0300
Tel: 609-452-2820
Email: newsfund@wsj.dowjones.com
http://djnewspaperfund.dowjones.com

The EFA is an organization for freelance editors. Members receive a newsletter and a free listing in their directory.

Editorial Freelancers Association (EFA)
71 West 23rd Street, Suite 1910
New York, NY 10010-4102
Tel: 866-929-5400
Email: info@the-efa.org
http://www.the-efa.org

For comprehensive information for citizens, students, and news people about the field of journalism, visit

Project for Excellence in Journalism and the Committee of Concerned Journalists
http://www.journalism.org

The Slot is a website founded and maintained by Bill Walsh, copy chief, national desk at the Washington Post. *Walsh's tips on proper*

word usage, grammar lessons, and style guides are not only inform-
ative, but also funny.

The Slot
http://www.theslot.com

═══════════ INTERVIEW ═══════════

Teresa Schmedding is a news editor at the Daily Herald. *As the fifth
fastest growing newspaper in the country, the* Daily Herald *has a circulation of 150,000 in the Chicago suburbs. Teresa has worked as a
journalist for 15 years. She was kind enough to discuss her career with
the editors of* Careers in Focus: Journalism.

Q. Why did you decide to become a newspaper editor?

A. I decided in high school I wanted to go into journalism. I won an
award—the Missouri State High School Journalist of the Year—
which came with a scholarship to the University of Missouri-
Columbia. But, I'll admit, it wasn't until a few years after college
that I knew I'd made the right choice. In high school, it can be
intimidating to have so many options—and to feel so insecure
about all of them. I wasn't sure for a long time if I went into newspapers because I really loved them, or if it was because someone said I was good at it. I knew a few years later, when I felt like
I was in the eye of a hurricane on deadline while chaos swirled
all around because of breaking news, that I knew I truly loved my
profession.

**Q. What are your primary and secondary job duties as a news
editor?**

A. I'm a department head who oversees a staff of 40+ copy editors
on the night, features, neighbor/day, and business desks. I also
work on some strategic planning committees. I work at night,
serving as the primary slot on major page-one stories and adjusting the paper as needed for breaking news, coordinating changes
with the press and distribution. My top priority as a news editor is to make sure our stories are fair, sensitive, and accurate.
If a story isn't ready to go and doesn't meet the ethical and quality standards of the *Daily Herald,* I won't put it in the paper.

**Q. How did you train for this job? What was your college
major?**

A. I majored in journalism at the University of Missouri-Columbia.
I started out as a reporter in college, but I switched to editing

and design after learning through Poynter's Eye Track studies how few people read past the headline of a story. I trained for this job by working on various desks at the *Daily Herald,* learning the paper's style and tone, along with basic operations. I also attended an American Press Institute Critical Management Skills seminar. It was very insightful and helped me greatly as I moved into management. I'm also currently enrolled at Mizzou, getting a master's in newspaper management. Also, when I was at Mizzou, I worked at a local TV station running camera for the 6:00 and 10:00 P.M. news. It was one of the most valuable experiences of my life. In broadcast, 30 seconds is an eternity. In newspapers, most think it isn't, but the lessons I learned about thinking on your feet and multi-tasking at that TV station have served me well in my current job.

Q. How/where did you get your first job in the field?

A. My first job was at the *Quad-City Times* in Davenport, Iowa. The news editor at the *Times* agreed to look over my material and offer me some career advice, but she offered me a job instead.

Q. What other journalism jobs have you held?

A. I was a copy editor at the *Quad-City Times,* then I was a dayside copy editor here at the *Daily Herald,* then I moved to nights, then I was metro news editor (a copy desk position), assistant news editor, night news editor, and then news editor.

Q. What are the most important professional qualities for news editors?

A. Patience and impatience. Tolerance and intolerance. You need to be able to work with a variety of people and know when to push an issue, a deadline, a story—and when not to. You need to be intolerant about shoddy work but able to tolerate reporters and editors working on a variety of skill levels. You cannot let your ego guide your decisions, and you must be self-motivated. You'll spend hours doing a thousand tasks to make the paper better, and, if you do your job right, no one will even notice so you won't get a lot of pats on the back or accolades from the public. But, when you do your job wrong, such as insert a typo or make an error in a headline, you'll be inundated with complaints.

Q. What are some of the pros and cons of your job?

A. I'm the final, objective eye before a story goes into print. I like to think I'm the moral and ethical backbone of the newspaper. One of the cons though, is sometimes you can only do so much from the tail end of the process. And the hours are rough. I'm lucky at the *Daily Herald* that the copy desk is viewed as a partner in the newsroom, not just a processing pagination machine. So if someone on my staff has serious concerns about a story, reporters and editors will work with them to make it better.

Another great aspect of my job is that I work for a family owned newspaper. I know the people who sign my paychecks. That affords me a greater degree of flexibility in my job than if I worked for a large conglomerate. I also know Paddock Publications is an honest publication that wouldn't lie about it's circulation, etc. That's why I've stayed here versus going to a larger paper.

My absolute favorite moments at work is when it feel like the world is falling apart. Someone was shot 10 minutes before deadline. Gore's president, then he's not. Michael Jordan might retire for the hundredth time. A tornado touches down. Directing reporters, photographers, copy editors, and production and somehow coming up with a sophisticated/responsible package in a matter of minutes is a true thrill. That's when you really rely on your instincts and your team.

Q. What advice would you give high school students who are interested in becoming newspaper journalists?

A. It's great to be interested in newspapers, but don't focus on it to the point that you lose sight of other things. The best journalists are those with a natural curiosity, who know a lot of things about a lot of different subjects. Too many journalists today are manipulated by savvy PR flaks and government officials. The more you know, the better you can interpret the news for readers—not just regurgitate jargon. For example, when editing a story, an editor on my staff flagged that using the term "Panzer movement" would be offensive (it's a Nazi tank maneuver). I'd also recommend picking a college with a broad-based journalism program, not just one with a student newspaper or magazine. You should take a course or two in broadcasting and advertising. The journalists of the future will be those who can cross over from one medium to the next and those with the best business sense. I also would encourage students to get involved in organizations now, such as the Young Journalists Association and the American Copy Editors Society. If you get involved now and make contacts with a few seasoned journalists, their advice and mentorship will serve you well throughout your career.

Desktop Publishing Specialists

QUICK FACTS

School Subjects
Art
Computer science
Journalism

Personal Skills
Artistic
Communication/ideas

Work Environment
Primarily indoors
Primarily one location

Minimum Education Level
Some postsecondary training

Salary Range
$18,600 to $31,590 to
$52,550+

Certification or Licensing
None available

Outlook
Faster than the average

DOT
979

GOE
01.06.01

NOC
1423

O*NET-SOC
43-9031.00

OVERVIEW

Desktop publishing specialists prepare computer files of text, graphics, and page layout for newspaper, magazine, and book publishers. They work with files others have created, or they compose original text and graphics using page layout programs. There are approximately 35,000 desktop publishing specialists employed in the United States, 14,000 of which are employed by newspaper, periodical, directory, and book publishers.

HISTORY

Johannes Gutenberg's invention of movable type in the 1440s was a major technological advancement in the history of printing. Up until that point, books were produced entirely by hand by monks, every word written in ink on vellum. Though print shops flourished after the invention of moveable type, inspiring the production of millions of books by the 1500s, there was no other major change in the technology of printing until the 1800s. By then, cylinder presses were churning out thousands of sheets per hour, and the Linotype machine allowed for easier, more efficient plate-making. Offset lithography (a method of applying ink from a treated surface onto paper) followed and gained popularity after World War II. Phototypesetting was later developed, involving creating film images of text and pictures to be printed.

At the end of the 20th century, computers caused another revolution in the industry. Desktop publishing software allows for the complete electronic design and production of newspapers, magazines, books, and other publications. This technology and the work of desktop publishing specialists save publishers significant amounts of time and money and have revolutionized the publishing and printing industries.

THE JOB

If you've ever used a computer to design and print a page in your high school paper or yearbook, then you've had some experience in desktop publishing. Not so many years ago, the prepress process (the steps to prepare a document for the printing press) involved metal casts, molten lead, light tables, knives, wax, paste, and a number of different professionals, from artists to typesetters. Desktop publishing technology has consolidated, and even eliminated, many of these positions and helped create the career of desktop publishing specialist.

Desktop publishing specialists have artistic talents—writing, editing, and proofreading skills—and a great deal of computer knowledge. They use the latest in design software—programs such as Photoshop, Illustrator, InDesign (all from software designer Adobe), and QuarkXpress—to format and prepare text, photographs, illustrations, and other graphical elements for publication. Once they create an electronic publication, desktop publishing specialists convert and prepare these files for printing presses and other media, such as the Internet and CD-ROM.

Typesetting and page layout work entails selecting font types and sizes, arranging column widths, checking for proper spacing between letters, words, and columns, placing graphics and pictures, and more. Desktop publishing specialists choose from the hundreds of typefaces available, taking the purpose and tone of the text into consideration when selecting from fonts with round shapes or long shapes, thick strokes or thin, serifs or sans serifs. They also use scanners to capture photographs, illustrations, or other types of art. These electronic images can then be placed into electronic page layouts or uploaded to a publisher's website.

Writing, editing, and proofreading are also important duties for desktop publishing specialists. Articles must be updated, or in some cases rewritten, before they are arranged on a page. They must also be proofread to ensure that no errors have been created during the layout process. Large newspapers and magazines may employ separate writers, editors, and proofreaders to handle these specific tasks.

Desktop publishing specialists deal with technical issues, such as resolution problems, colors that need to be corrected, and software difficulties. An art director or editor may come in with a hand-drawn sketch, a printout of a design, or a file on a CD, and he or she may want the piece ready to be quickly posted on the newspaper's online edition or to be published in the next issue of a newspaper or magazine. Each format presents different issues, and desktop publishing specialists must be familiar with the processes and solutions for each.

Some desktop publishing specialists may work with multimedia elements (such as video, film, audio, or animation). These elements might be used to make a basic news story at the publisher's website more interesting to the reader.

REQUIREMENTS

High School

Classes that will help you develop desktop publishing skills include computer science, design, and art. Computer classes should include both hardware and software instruction, since understanding how computers function will help you with troubleshooting and knowing a computer's limits. Through photography classes you can learn about composition, color, and design elements. Typing, drafting, and print shop classes, if available, will also provide you with the opportunity to gain some indispensable skills. Working on the school newspaper or yearbook will train you on desktop publishing skills as well, including page layout, typesetting, composition, and working under a deadline.

Postsecondary Training

Although a college degree is not a prerequisite, many desktop publishing specialists have a certificate or a bachelor's degree. Areas of study range from English to graphic design. Some two-year colleges and technical institutes offer programs in desktop publishing or related fields. A growing number of schools offer programs in technical and visual communications, which may include classes in desktop publishing, layout and design, and computer graphics. Four-year colleges also offer courses in technical communications and graphic design. You can enroll in classes related to desktop publishing through extended education programs offered through universities and colleges. These classes, often taught by professionals in the industry, cover basic desktop publishing techniques and advanced lessons on software programs such as Adobe Photoshop or QuarkXPress.

Additionally, the Association of Graphic Communications (AGC) offers an electronic publishing certificate program that covers the following topics: electronic publishing introduction, Acrobat and

PDF technologies, color theory, graphic design, Illustrator, InDesign, Photoshop, QuarkXPress, prepress and preflight, print production, proofreading and copyediting, electronic publishing, scanning, and typography and font management. Contact the AGC for more information.

Other Requirements

Desktop publishing specialists are detail-oriented, possess problem-solving skills, and have a sense of design and artistic skills.

A good eye and patience are critical, as is the endurance to see projects through to completion. You should have an aptitude for computers, the ability to type quickly and accurately, and a natural curiosity. In addition, a calm temperament comes in handy when working under pressure and constant deadlines. You should be flexible and be able to handle more than one project at a time. You should also be able to work with a variety of publishing industry professionals, including art directors, illustrators, photographers, writers, and editors.

EXPLORING

Experimenting with your home computer, or a computer at school or the library, will give you a good idea as to whether desktop publishing is for you. Play around with various graphic design and page layout programs. If you subscribe to an Internet service, take advantage of any free Web space available to you and design your own home page. Join computer clubs and volunteer to produce newsletters and flyers for school or community clubs. Volunteering is an excellent way to try new software and techniques as well as gain experience troubleshooting and creating final products. Part-time or summer employment with newspaper and magazine publishers is a great way to gain experience and make valuable contacts.

EMPLOYERS

Approximately 14,000 desktop publishing specialists are employed by newspaper, magazine, directory, and book publishers throughout the United States. Other employers of desktop publishing specialists include printing companies and shops, advertising agencies, and graphic design agencies. Some large companies also contract with desktop publishing services rather than hire full-time designers. Government agencies hire desktop publishing specialists for the large number of documents they publish. The U.S. Government Printing

Office has a Digital Information Technology Support Group that provides desktop and electronic publishing services to federal agencies.

STARTING OUT

Most desktop publishing specialists enter the field through either the production side or the editorial side of the industry. Those with training as a designer or artist can easily master the finer techniques of production. Publishing companies often hire desktop publishing specialists to work in-house or as freelance employees. Working within the industry, you can make connections and build up a clientele.

You can also start out by investing in computer hardware and software, and volunteering your services. By designing logos, letterhead, and newsletters, for example, your work will gain quick recognition, and word of your services will spread.

ADVANCEMENT

Desktop publishing specialists advance by taking on larger projects or moving from small publishers to larger publishers. They may also decide to start their own businesses.

EARNINGS

There is limited salary information available for desktop publishing specialists, most likely because the job duties of desktop publishing specialists can vary and often overlap with other jobs. Entry-level desktop publishing specialists with little or no experience generally earn minimum wage. Freelancers can earn from $15 to $100 an hour.

According to the U.S. Department of Labor, median annual earnings of desktop publishing specialists were $31,590 in 2003. Salaries ranged from less than $18,600 to $52,550 or more a year. Desktop publishing specialists who were employed by newspaper, periodical, directory, and book publishers had mean annual earnings of $30,520 in 2003. Wage rates vary depending on experience, training, region, and size of the publisher.

WORK ENVIRONMENT

Desktop publishing specialists spend most of their time working in front of a computer, whether editing text, scanning images, laying out pages, or preparing files for the printer or the Web. Hours may vary depending on project deadlines at hand. Many newspapers are published daily, while magazines may be published weekly, bimonthly, or monthly. Projects range from laying out a section of a daily newspaper, to preparing electronic files of an entire magazine for the printer, to working on content for a newspaper's online edition.

OUTLOOK

According to the U.S. Department of Labor, employment for desktop publishing specialists is projected to grow faster than the average through 2012. As technology advances, the ability to create and publish documents will become easier and faster, thus influencing more businesses to produce printed materials. Desktop publishing specialists will be needed to satisfy typesetting, page layout, design, and editorial demands.

QuarkXPress, Adobe InDesign, Macromedia FreeHand, Adobe Illustrator, and Adobe Photoshop are some programs often used in desktop publishing. Specialists with experience in these and other software will be in demand.

FOR MORE INFORMATION

For information on the electronic publishing certificate program, contact

Association of Graphic Communications
330 Seventh Avenue, 9th Floor
New York, NY 10001-5010
Tel: 212-279-2100
Email: info@agcomm.org
http://www.agcomm.org

This organization is a source of financial support for education and research projects designed to promote careers in graphic communications. For more information, contact

Graphic Arts Education and Research Foundation
1899 Preston White Drive
Reston, VA 20191
Tel: 866-381-9839
Email: gaerf@npes.org
http://www.gaerf.org

This organization offers information, services, and training related to printing, electronic prepress, electronic publishing, and other areas of the graphic arts industry.

Graphic Arts Information Network
Graphic Arts Technical Foundation/Printing Industries of
America
200 Deer Run Road
Sewickley, PA 15143-2600
Tel: 800-910-4283
Email: info@gatf.org
http://www.gain.net

For industry statistics, information on diversity, and to view a Powerpoint presentation entitled "Tips on Finding a Job in Magazines" visit the MPA website.

Magazine Publishers of America (MPA)
810 Seventh Avenue, 24th Floor
New York, NY 10019
Email: mpa@magazine.org
http://www.magazine.org

Visit this NASAD website for information on schools.

National Association of Schools of Art and Design (NASAD)
11250 Roger Bacon Drive, Suite 21
Reston, VA 20190-5248
Tel: 703-437-0700
Email: info@arts-accredit.org
http://nasad.arts-accredit.org

For information on careers in newspapers and industry facts and figures, contact

Newspaper Association of America
1921 Gallows Road, Suite 600
Vienna, VA 22182-3900
Tel: 703-902-1600
Email: IRC@naa.org
http://www.naa.org

For information on educational programs, contact

Society for Technical Communication
901 North Stuart Street, Suite 904
Arlington, VA 22203-1822
Tel: 703-522-4114

Email: stc@stc.org
http://www.stc.org

For information on careers and educational institutions, visit
Graphic Comm Central
http://teched.vt.edu/gcc

———————————— INTERVIEW ————————————

Yuan-Kwan Chan is an online producer for the New York Times *on the Web. She was kind enough to discuss her career with the editors of* Careers in Focus: Journalism.

Q. How long have you worked in journalism?

A. My journalism experience, mostly in print and online media, spans more than a decade. I have spent the past four years as an online producer and am currently employed at the *New York Times* on the Web.

Q. Please briefly describe your primary responsibilities as an online producer.

A. As a producer, I am responsible for the nightly translation of the print edition of the newspaper into online format. On average, I produce about two to four dozen stories in a given evening. I take the copy that has filtered into our system and make it presentable for the website, add features such as links or related keywords (so that our articles will show up in searches and archives), and decide whether advertisements should be turned off if the article topic is sensitive. If an enterprise story has strong art and includes more photo possibilities than the newspaper has room for, I will work with our multimedia producers to piece together a slide show with about a dozen photos or so. Longer enterprise pieces sometimes work well with video or an audio slide show (a number of photos juxtaposed with an audio voiceover, usually by the reporter, or one or more of the interview subjects). I also work with the newspaper to develop special sections for major events such as the Republican and Democratic National Conventions, and I arrange Q&A sessions between reporters and registered online readers.

My primary beat is sports, which requires me to make more business decisions than producers at other desks. Our sports sections include statistics pages with scoreboards, team rosters, and other live updates, all of which are provided by various vendors. Throughout the year, I am contacted by potential advertisers and sponsors for our ongoing special event coverage (i.e., Super Bowl, Tour de France). For these duties, I work with the advertising and technical departments, assess our vendors, and make decisions as to whether the dotted line should be signed or whether our money would be better spent elsewhere.

Q. **What are the major challenges with presenting print copy on the Web? How are the two audiences (print versus electronic) different?**

A. A print audience is smaller and more regionally focused than an electronic audience. There are also space limitations in a newspaper, whereas on the Web, this is not the case. The immediate challenge is to present copy that is engaging to the reader. A hard copy of an article can be folded up, saved for later, and processed bit by bit. A Web version must combine the best of traditional media: broadcast in the sense that information must be presented in a way that is not too hard on readers' eyes staring at a monitor, print and photojournalism in that layout and design are key elements for presenting that information, and all media for any photo, video, and audio elements that accompany an article.

Another challenge with presenting print copy online is that different readers have different connections (modem versus broadband), browsers (Netscape versus Internet Explorer) and software programs (RealPlayer versus QuickTime). What may look perfectly fine on one person's screen may not translate well to another.

Q. **What did you study in college, and do you feel it prepared you for your career?**

A. I received my bachelor of business administration degree from the College of William & Mary with a concentration in marketing and minor in music. This degree included a year of management courses at the University of Manchester Institute of Science & Technology in England. I subsequently earned a master of science in journalism, specializing in online media, from Northwestern University.

Combined with volunteerism opportunities, freelance assignments, and numerous internships in journalism and other fields, both degrees prepared me well for my career. I continue to draw from my studies to this day, and I would advise all students to not limit one's academics and extracurricular activities to journalism-related endeavors. I was able to enter sports media not because I was an athlete—far from it!—but because I took a sports marketing class in the M.B.A. program at Northwestern's Kellogg School of Management, completed an internship with a Chicago tennis tournament, and volunteered at numerous sporting events over the years. I could also relate very well to the lifestyle that athletes were going through thanks to my 13 years of classical piano studies and competitions, and this bond helped me in my interviews. At the same time, I pursued my interests in journalism by writing for a number of publications, including the (Minneapolis) *Star Tribune,* Tribune Media Services, and the *Seattle Post-Intelligencer* as a Dow Jones Newspaper Fund business reporting scholarship winner trained by the *Wall Street Journal.* I strongly believe that if one pursues many interests, one will find that a more interdisciplinary approach will stand one in good stead for a versatile journalism career.

Q. How/where did you get your first job as an online producer?

A. At first, I thought I was lucky. I mailed—not e-mailed, but actually dropped in the mailbox—my materials to the general human resources department at CNN Interactive. A manager there contacted me, and I was soon on my way to Atlanta. However, I quickly realized that this opportunity stemmed from years of developing important contacts, aligning myself with professional journalism organizations, and networking.

Q. What are the most important personal and professional qualities for online producers?

A. The ability to multitask and prioritize is very important. Unlike print, where deadlines usually come at a specific date and time, the mentality in online media is "ASAP." For example, on most given nights, I am the sole producer responsible for the content on every sports section on the website. I might be working on a small story for the tennis subsection, but if a major story breaks, I have to be prepared to drop what I'm working on and focus on a new task. Fortunately, top-level editors at print publications are beginning to see that they can still break news even after the printing presses have closed. As long as reporters are equipped with email access or a mobile phone, their copy can be sent to the website and posted in minutes because we will always have at least one person in the office. This was particularly vital to our Iraq war coverage with reporters filing from different time zones.

Also, teamwork and collaboration are very important to the success of a website, more so than a print publication where reporters often have specific beats. Despite our respective titles and desks, producers often have to wear a number of hats and be prepared to take over duties that are not regularly ours should the need arise. For myself, that has included working on national and political news on at least a weekly basis, and pitching in to help on New York region stories and op-eds.

Q. What are some of the pros and cons of your job?

A. One huge pro is that I have a lot of autonomy with my job. While top editors hold daily meetings to decide which stories should make it to the front page of their respective newspapers, I make those editorial decisions on my own with the click of a mouse. In addition, despite the fact that *The Times's* website is linked to a print entity, I am not necessarily bound to the editorial decisions of the newspaper, particularly since their publication closes at 1:00 or 2:00 A.M., whereas our website is a 24-hours-a-day, 7-days-a-week operation.

That said, the hours of our jobs are unpredictable. It is rare that, at the editorial level, schedules fall into a neat Monday to Friday, 9-to-5 routine. One of my colleagues, for example, works from 6:00 A.M., to 2:00 P.M., whereas my shift is regularly 6:00 P.M. to 2:00 A.M.! Since I am a city person, this is not a big issue in New York. But in other parts of the country, this could have a huge damper on one's personal life when establishments have closed long before work shifts are over.

Q. What advice would you give high school students who are interested in becoming online producers?

A. I would suggest that students look into creating personal websites in order to experiment with design, HTML coding, and Flash. These websites can not only be online publications—therefore enhancing a student's portfolio—but also serve as a recruiting tool. Another avenue is an existing online publication, such as the website of a school newspaper. If one doesn't exist, then create it! Become familiar with software programs such as Adobe Photoshop, HomeSite, and DreamWeaver. Finally, I would study and critique other major news websites to see what works and what doesn't in terms of templates, design, editorial presentation, photos, and so forth.

Q. What is the future of your job? How will it change in the near future?

A. The future of my job depends very heavily on the development of broadband technology and people's access to it. Right now, our audio and video capabilities with multimedia are severely restricted by the reality that access to the best technological tools is not widespread or mainstream. Therefore, the quality of a multimedia project can differ greatly between two computers with different browsers, platforms, and connection speeds.

Aside from the technological aspect, I think that we will see more automation for mundane tasks such as story production, and more original reporting in the field.

Q. How will Web journalism change over the next decade?

A. Going back to the previous question, I think that we will see more original reporting from producers and editors. Web journalists must draw from all traditional media; today's Web journalist already has to have the reporting and writing skills, the ability to simultaneously present and think in broadcast and print terms, and the capability to navigate through a number of software programs. I also feel that we will see more and more online niche publications start from scratch and develop into viable business entities. The development of Web journalism has already had major effects on traditional media, and I think that trend will continue.

Editorial and Research Assistants

QUICK FACTS

School Subjects
English
Journalism

Personal Interests
Communication/ideas
Following instructions

Work Environment
Primarily indoors
Primarily one location

Minimum Education Level
Some postsecondary training

Salary Range
$20,000 to $30,400 to
$40,000+

Certification or Licensing
None available

Outlook
About as fast as the average

DOT
132

GOE
11.08.01

NOC
1452, 4122

O*NET-SOC
27-3041.00

OVERVIEW

Editorial and research assistants perform a wide range of functions, but their primary responsibility is to assist editors with ensuring that text provided by writers is accurate and suitable in content, format, and style for the intended audiences. Editorial and research assistants work for magazines, newspapers, book publishers, newsletters, corporations of all kinds, advertising agencies, radio stations, television stations, and Internet sites.

HISTORY

For as long as newspapers, magazines, and books have been published, editorial and research assistants have helped editors and other publishing professionals to fact check, proofread, and otherwise ensure that articles and other text are appropriate for publication. Although these positions are entry level in nature, they offer an excellent introduction to the world of publishing. Many top journalists and editors broke into the business as editorial and research assistants.

Today's editorial and research assistants use computers and the Internet to help them do their jobs more quickly and effectively. They remain key support workers in publishing, journalism, broadcasting, and other industries.

THE JOB

Editorial and research assistants work for many kinds of publishers, publications, and corporations. They assist editors with the tasks necessary to provide clearly written, accurate reading material. Both positions tend to be entry-level jobs that may provide the opportunity for advancement. Editorial and research assistants may be assigned to support one editor or writer, an editorial team, or an entire department. They may work on one project at a time or several projects simultaneously.

Editorial assistants perform many different tasks. They may handle the clerical aspects of an editorial project, such as going through the editorial department mail, filing documents, making photocopies, corresponding with authors, and submitting expense reports and invoices to accounting for payment. They may be responsible for obtaining permission to reuse previously published materials such as artwork, maps, tables, or writing from another person, or verifying that the author has already obtained permission. They may also perform other tasks more directly involved with editing, such as reviewing text for style and format issues, correcting any spelling or grammar errors, and adding or deleting content to make the text more readable or to adhere to space specifications. They may be responsible for using desktop publishing software to take editorial elements such as text, photos, or art and create page layouts.

In addition to the tasks mentioned above, some editorial assistants who work with artists and photographers are responsible for writing captions for photographs or labels for artwork. Editorial assistants who work for newspapers may perform basic and formulaic tasks such as updating the winning lottery numbers, sports scores, or calendar events listed in the newspaper, or they may undertake simple writing assignments such as creating birth, engagement, wedding, or anniversary announcements, or obituaries. Editorial assistants who work for book publishers may be responsible for reading through unsolicited manuscripts from writers and determining, which editor, if any, it should be forwarded to for further consideration.

Research assistants generally perform research tasks such as verifying the dates, facts, names of persons and places, and statistics used by a writer. They may review a writer's sources and then verify that the information provided by these sources is correct. They may contact any persons interviewed by the writer to ensure that any quotes used by the writer are truthful and correct. Research assistants also contact experts in subject areas pertaining to the topic of the article, often to obtain additional information for the writer, or verify information already used in the article. If a research assistant finds any errors or discrepancies with the writer's text, they are expected to flag and correct them. A research assistant may meet with the writer and/or editor to discuss any dis-crepancies that are not easily resolved.

Research assistants use a variety of tools to do their jobs. They rely on telephones, fax machines, and computers to obtain the information they need. Researchers may utilize libraries, the Internet, and in-house collections of information as sources of facts, figures, and statistics. Although they may work in a variety of settings, many research assistants work in the magazine/periodical publishing industry.

REQUIREMENTS

High School

Editorial and research assistants must be expert communicators, so you should excel in English. You must learn to write extremely well, since you will be correcting and even rewriting the work of others. If elective classes in writing are available in your school, take them. Take journalism and communications courses. Work as a writer or editor for the school paper. Since virtually all editorial and research assistants use computers, take computer courses and learn how to type quickly and accurately.

Postsecondary Training

Most employers require an editorial assistant to have at least two years of college, and a bachelor's degree is preferred, especially if you wish to advance to a higher position. Research assistants should also have a bachelor's degree. Most editorial workers have degrees in English or journalism, but it is not unheard of to major in one of the other liberal arts. If you know that you want to specialize in a spe-cific field—for example, scientific editing—you may wish to major in an area of science while minoring in English, writing, or journalism. Many colleges offer courses in book editing, magazine design, gen-eral editing, and writing. Some colleges, such as the University of Chicago, University of Denver, and Stanford University, offer pro-grams in publishing.

While in college, work on the school paper, literary magazine, or yearbook staff. Many magazines and newspapers offer internships to students interested in editorial work. Find a part-time job with a newspaper or magazine, even if it is a non-editorial position. Take advantage of these opportunities. Everything you can learn about the publishing business will help you find a job later.

Other Requirements

Good editorial and research assistants are fanatics for the written word. They read a lot, across many topics, and know how to think clearly and communicate what they are thinking. When they are curious about something, they take action and research the subject. They are not satisfied with not knowing things.

You must be detail-oriented to succeed as an editorial or research assistant. You must also be patient, since you may have to spend hours to painstakingly track down hard-to-find facts and figures. You must be good not only at identifying problems but also at solving them, so you must be creative.

EXPLORING

One of the best ways to explore the editorial and research field is to work for a school newspaper or other publication. Being involved in researching, writing, reporting, proofreading, page layout, printing, or any other task will help you to understand editing and research and how they relate to the entire field of publishing. If you cannot work for the school paper, try to land a part-time job with a local newspaper or newsletter.

Another way to explore the field is by writing, since editing and writing are inextricably linked. You can try keeping a journal, or try other kinds of writing, such as letters to the editor, short stories, poetry, essays, comedic prose, and plays. Write something every day. Try to rework your writing until it is as good as you can make it. This will give you a feel for what an editorial worker does.

EMPLOYERS

One of the best things about the fields of editing and research is that there are many kinds of employment opportunities. The most obvious employers for editorial and research assistants are newspapers, magazines, and book publishers. Most publishers are located in New York City, but many other publishers can be found in large cities across the country. Other employers of editorial and research assistants include advertising agencies; colleges and universities; corporations; museums; nonprofit organizations; local, state, and federal governments; and radio and television news stations.

STARTING OUT

The positions of editorial assistant and research assistant are great opportunities to get your foot in the door of the editorial world. There is tremendous competition for editorial jobs, so it is important for a beginner who wishes to break into the business to be as well prepared

Career Paths for Journalism Majors, 2002

Since 1964, graduates of bachelor degree programs in journalism and mass communication have been surveyed by several newspaper organizations and colleges (including the University of Georgia's Grady College of Journalism and Mass Communication, which took over the survey in 1997) about, among other issues, their employment status six months after graduation. To be included in the survey, graduates must have received their degrees from one of the programs in journalism and mass communication listed in either the Dow Jones Newspaper Fund's *Journalism Career and Scholarship Guide* or the *Journalism and Mass Communication Directory*, which is published by the Association for Education in Journalism and Mass Communication. The following chart details career paths for 2002 graduates of journalism and mass communication programs.

Career Path	Percent Entering Field
Book publishers	0.5
Magazine publishers	1.3
Radio, television, and cable television broadcasting	8.1
Newspapers and news services	8.3
Continued education	8.4
Public relations and advertising	8.7
Unemployed	16.2
Other communications careers	23.6
Noncommunications careers	24.9

Source: University of Georgia, Grady College of Journalism and Mass Communication, Annual Survey of Journalism & Mass Communications Graduates, 2002

as possible. College students who have gained experience as interns, have worked for publications during the summers, or have attended special programs in publishing will be at an advantage. Applicants for editorial positions must also expect to take and pass tests that are designed to determine their language skills.

Good sources of information about job openings are school placement offices, classified ads in newspapers and trade journals, specialized publications such as *Publishers Weekly* (http://publishersweekly.com), and Internet sites. One way to proceed is to identify local publishers through the yellow pages. Many publishers have websites that list job openings, and large publishers often have telephone job lines that serve the same purpose.

ADVANCEMENT

Employees who start as editorial assistants and show promise generally become *editors* or *copy editors.* After gaining skill in that position, they may be given a wider range of duties while retaining the same title. The next step may be a position as an *assistant editor* or *associate editor,* and then *senior editor.* Copy editors may advance to a position such as *senior copy editor,* which involves overseeing the work of junior copy editors. Editors and copy editors may also progress to the position of *project editor.* The project editor performs a wide variety of tasks, including copyediting, coordinating the work of in-house and freelance copy editors, and managing the schedule of a particular project. From this position, a typical line of advancement for an editor may be to move up to become *first assistant editor,* then *managing editor,* then *editor in chief.* These positions involve more management and decision making than is usually found in the positions described previously. The editor in chief works with the publisher to ensure that a suitable editorial policy is being followed, while the managing editor is responsible for all aspects of the editorial department. The assistant editor provides support to the managing editor.

Employees who start as research assistants usually have the same advancement options of editorial assistants, or they may choose to advance within the research department, taking on greater responsibilities and earning a higher salary. Some research assistants, as well as editorial assistants, branch out into careers in writing.

In many cases, editorial workers advance by moving from a position in one company to the same position with a larger or more prestigious company. Such moves may bring significant increases in both pay and status.

EARNINGS

Competition for editorial jobs is fierce, and there is no shortage of people who wish to enter the field. For that reason, companies that employ editorial and research assistants generally pay relatively low wages.

A *Publishers Weekly* salary survey reported that editorial assistant salaries in 2003 ranged from $28,378 at smaller companies to

$30,400 at large publishing houses. However, beginning salaries of $20,000 or less are still common in many places.

Earnings of research assistants vary widely, depending on the level of education and the experience of the research assistant and employer. Generally, large companies pay research assistants more than smaller companies and nonprofit organizations do. Self-employed research assistants get paid by the hour or by assignment. Depending on the experience of the research assistant, the complexity of the assignment, and the location of the job, pay rates may be anywhere from $7 to $25 per hour, although $10 to $12 is the norm.

WORK ENVIRONMENT

The environments in which editorial and research assistants work can vary widely. For the most part, publishers of all kinds realize that a quiet atmosphere is conducive to work that requires tremendous concentration. Most editorial and research assistants work in cubicles. Editorial and research assistants in publishing often work in quieter surroundings than do assistants working for a newspaper or in advertising agencies, who sometimes work in rather loud and hectic situations.

Even in relatively quiet surroundings, however, editorial and research assistants often have many distractions. While working on assignment, an assistant may also have to deal with phone calls from authors, meetings with members of the editorial and production staff, and questions from freelancers, among many other details.

Deadlines are an important issue for all editorial workers. Newspaper and magazine editorial and research assistants face daily or weekly deadlines, whereas those who are employed by book publishers usually have deadlines that are months in length. In almost all cases, though, editorial and research assistants must work long hours during certain phases of the editing process to meet deadlines.

OUTLOOK

According to the *Occupational Outlook Handbook*, employment of editorial workers such as editorial and research assistants will increase about as fast as the average through 2012. At the same time, however, competition for those jobs will remain intense, since so many people want to enter the field. Much of the expansion in publishing is expected to occur in newspapers, periodicals, book publishers, nonprofit organizations, online publications, and advertising and public relations.

FOR MORE INFORMATION

The following organization's website is an excellent source of information about careers in editing. The ACES organizes educational seminars and maintains lists of internships.

American Copy Editors Society (ACES)
3 Healy Street
Huntington, NY 11743
http://www.copydesk.org

This organization of book publishers offers an extensive website to learn about the book business.

Association of American Publishers
71 Fifth Avenue, Second Floor
New York, NY 10003
Tel: 212-255-0200
http://www.publishers.org

This organization provides information about internships and about the newspaper business in general.

Dow Jones Newspaper Fund
PO Box 300
Princeton, NJ 08543-0300
Tel: 609-452-2820
Email: newsfund@wsj.dowjones.com
http://djnewspaperfund.dowjones.com/fund

This organization is a good source of information on internships.

Magazine Publishers of America
810 Seventh Avenue, 24th Floor
New York, NY 10019
Tel: 212-872-3700
http://www.magazine.org

The Slot is a website founded and maintained by Bill Walsh, financial copy desk chief at the Washington Post. *Walsh's tips on proper word usage, grammar lessons, and style guides are not only informative, but also funny.*

The Slot
http://www.theslot.com

Fashion Writers and Editors

QUICK FACTS

School Subjects
English
Family and consumer science
Journalism

Personal Skills
Artistic
Communication/ideas

Work Environment
Primarily indoors
One location with some
travel

Minimum Education Level
Bachelor's degree

Salary Range
$20,000 to $38,000 to
$100,000+ (writers)
$20,000 to $47,260 to
$77,430+ (editors)

Certification or Licensing
None available

Outlook
About as fast as the average

DOT
131, 132

GOE
01.01.01, 01.01.02

NOC
5121, 5122

O*NET-SOC
27-3041.00, 27-3043.00

OVERVIEW

Fashion writers express, promote, and interpret fashion ideas and facts in written form. *Fashion editors* perform a wide range of functions, but their primary responsibility is to ensure that text provided by fashion writers is suitable in content, format, and style for the intended audiences.

HISTORY

Starting around the 14th century, fashion trends were promoted via word of mouth and the exchange of fashion dolls. The development of the printing press by Johannes Gutenberg in the middle of the 15th century fostered the growth of printing publications, which eventually lead to publications dedicated to fashion. The first fashion magazine is generally thought to be a German publication that began in the late 16th century.

Fashion writers and editors were originally employed by newspaper, magazine, and book publishers. As technologies changed, fashion writers and editors began to discuss fashion on television and radio shows. Today, fashion writers and editors have a presence on the Web, as well.

THE JOB

Fashion writers, also known as *fashion reporters, correspondents,* or *authors,* express their ideas about fashion in words for books, magazines, newspapers, advertisements, radio, television, and the Internet. These writing jobs require a combination of creativity and hard work.

The majority of fashion writers are employed by fashion magazines. These writers report on fashion news, conduct interviews of top designers, or write feature articles on the latest styles for a season. Fashion writers also work for newspapers with fashion sections (often a part of a larger arts-and-entertainment department), websites, or other media outlets.

Good fashion writers gather as much information as possible about their subject and then carefully check the accuracy of their sources. This can involve extensive library research, interviews, and long hours of observation and personal experience. Writers usually keep notes from which they prepare an outline or summary. They use this outline to write a first draft and then rewrite sections of their material, always searching for the best way to express their ideas. Generally, their writing will be reviewed, corrected, and revised many times before a final copy is ready for publication.

Fashion editors work with fashion writers on the staffs on newspapers, magazines, publishing houses, radio or television stations, and corporations of all kinds. Their primary responsibility is to make sure that text provided by fashion writers is suitable in content, format, and style for the intended audiences. For example, a fashion editor working for a newspaper would ensure that articles are timely and can be understood and enjoyed by the newspaper's average reader—not just people in the fashion industry.

Editors must make sure that all text to be printed is well written, factually correct (sometimes this job is done by a *researcher* or *fact checker*), and grammatically correct. Other editors, including *managing editors, editors in chief,* and *editorial directors,* have managerial responsibilities and work with heads of other departments, such as marketing, sales, and production.

REQUIREMENTS

High School

Fashion writers and editors must learn to write well, so it is important to take English, journalism, and communications courses in high school. To gain a better perspective on fashion and design, take classes in family and consumer science, including sewing and design, if they are available in your school. Since much of the fashion industry is based overseas, taking classes in a foreign language, such as French, will also be beneficial. Since all editors and writers use computers, take computer courses and learn how to type quickly and accurately.

Books to Read

Brogan, Kathryn S., and Robert Lee Brewer, eds. *2005 Writer's Market.* Cincinnati, Ohio: Writers Digest Books, 2004.

Calasibetta, Charlotte Mankey. *The Fairchild Dictionary of Fashion.* London: Laurence King Publishing, 2003.

Dickerson, Kitty G., and Jeannette Jarnow. *Inside the Fashion Business.* 7th ed. Upper Saddle River, N.J.: Prentice Hall, 2002.

Mauro, Lucia, Kathy Siebel, and Maureen Costello. *Careers for Fashion Plates & Other Trendsetters.* 2d ed. New York: McGraw-Hill/Contemporary Books, 2002.

O'Hara Callan, Georgina. *The Thames and Hudson Dictionary of Fashion and Fashion Designers.* Rev. ed. New York: Thames & Hudson, 1998.

Postsecondary Training

A college education is usually necessary if you want to become a writer or editor. You should also know how to use a computer for word processing and be able to handle the pressure of deadlines. Employers prefer to hire people who have a communications, English, or journalism degree. Fashion writers and editors must be knowledgeable about their subject, so classes—or even degrees—in fashion design and marketing are also strongly recommended.

Other Requirements

Good fashion editors and writers are analytical people who know how to think clearly and communicate what they are thinking. They must have the ability to conceptualize in two and three dimensions and convey this information to their audience. They are benefited by a working knowledge of clothing construction and an eye for fashion trends. Fashion editors and writers must keep abreast of the latest styles and movements in the fashion industry.

EXPLORING

To improve your writing skills, read as much as you can. Read all kinds of writing—not just fashion articles. Fiction, nonfiction, poetry, and essays will introduce you to many different forms of writing.

Try to write every day. Write your own reviews or articles about the latest fashions or trends in the industry. You can also work as a reporter, writer, or editor on school newspapers, yearbooks, and literary magazines.

EMPLOYERS

Fashion writers and editors are typically employed by newspaper, magazine, and book publishers; radio and television stations; and online publications. Some fashion writers and editors are also employed by fashion houses and advertising agencies. In the United States, New York City, San Francisco, and Los Angeles are major fashion centers. Work also may be found in other U.S. cities, although not as many jobs are available in these locations. Many fashion positions are available in foreign countries.

STARTING OUT

Many fashion writers and editors start out in the industry by gaining experience as an editorial assistant. Typically, an editorial assistant who performs well will be given the opportunity to take on more and more editorial or writing duties as time passes.

The competition for editorial jobs is great, especially in the fashion industry, so it is important for a beginner who wishes to break into the business to be as well prepared as possible. College students who have gained experience as interns, have worked for fashion publications during the summers, or have attended special programs in publishing will be at an advantage.

Jobs may be found through your school's career services office, classified ads in newspapers and trade journals, specialized publications such as *Publishers Weekly* (http://publishersweekly.com), and Internet sites. Many publishers have websites that list job openings, and large publishers often have telephone job lines that serve the same purpose.

ADVANCEMENT

Employees who start as editorial assistants and show promise may be given a wider range of duties while retaining the same title. Eventually they may become editors or staff writers. They may progress from less significant stories and tasks to important fashion news and feature stories. As they accrue experience, they may be promoted to other editorial or writing positions that come with greater responsibility and pay. They may also choose to pursue managerial positions within the field of fashion editing and writing, such as managing editor and editor in chief. These positions involve more management and decision making than is usually found in the positions described previously. The editor in chief works with the publisher to ensure that a suitable editorial policy is being followed, while the managing editor is responsible for all aspects of the editorial department.

As is the case within many editorial and writing positions, a fashion writer or editor may advance by moving from a position on one publication or company to the same position with a larger or more prestigious publication or company. Such moves may involve an increase in both salary and prestige.

EARNINGS

Beginning fashion writers' salaries range from $20,000 to $26,000 per year. More experienced writers may earn between $28,000 and $38,000. Best-selling authors may make well $100,000 or more per year, but they are few in number.

The salaries of fashion editors are roughly comparable to those of other editors. Median annual earnings for all editors were $41,460 in 2003, according to the U.S. Department of Labor. The lowest 10 percent earned less than $24,590 and the highest 10 percent earned $77,430 or more. In 2003, the mean annual earnings for all editors in newspaper and book publishing were $47,260, while those employed in radio and television broadcasting earned $41,680. Starting salaries of $20,000 or less are still common in many areas.

WORK ENVIRONMENT

The environments in which fashion writers and editors work can vary widely. Most writers and editors work in offices or cubicles. But they many not spend all of their time there, as their job may require them to attend fashion shows in other cities, visit fashion houses or department stores, attend social functions, or make less glamorous visits to the library for research. Many of these events happen after the typical 9-to-5 workday is over, or on weekends.

Almost all fashion writers and editors must deal with deadlines, which affects their work environment. Some writers and editors, such as those who work for newspapers or magazines, work in a much more pressurized atmosphere than those working on books because they face daily or weekly deadlines. Fashion editors and writers working on books may have a more regular 40-hour work-week and less constant deadline pressure, since book production usually takes place over several months. In almost all cases, though, fashion writers and editors will work long hours during certain phases of the editing process to meet deadlines.

OUTLOOK

Employment opportunities in writing and editing are expected to increase about as fast as the average for all occupations through 2012, according to the U.S. Department of Labor. However, because of the narrow scope of fashion writing and editing, competition for jobs will be very intense. Individuals with previous experience and specialized education in fashion and reporting will be the most successful at finding jobs.

FOR MORE INFORMATION

This organization of book publishers offers an extensive website for people interested in learning more about the book business.
Association of American Publishers
71 Fifth Avenue, Second Floor
New York, NY 10003
Tel: 212-255-0200
http://www.publishers.org

For information on the industry, student membership, or networking opportunities, contact
Fashion Group International Inc.
8 West 40th Street, 7th Floor
New York, NY 10018
Tel: 212-302-5511
Email: info@fgi.org
http://www.fgi.org

This organization is a good source of information on internships and the magazine industry.
Magazine Publishers of America
810 Seventh Avenue, 24th Floor
New York, NY 10019
Email: mpa@magazine.org
http://www.magazine.org

For information on educational programs in fashion, contact
National Association of Schools of Art and Design
11250 Roger Bacon Drive, Suite 21
Reston, VA 20190-5248
Tel: 703-437-0700
Email: info@arts-accredit.org
http://nasad.arts-accredit.org

Visit this site for information on careers in fashion writing and editing and school listings.
Fashion-Schools.org
http://www.fashion-schools.org

To read about fashions, models, and agencies, check out this website hosted by fashion magazines Vogue *and* W.
Style.com
http://www.style.com

For subscription information, contact
Women's Wear Daily
http://www.wwd.com

Food Writers
and Editors

OVERVIEW

Food writers write about food and drink. They may report on food- or cooking-related events, interview chefs or other food/cooking personalities, review recipes or restaurants, or simply write about a specific food or product. With their writing, they may persuade the general public to choose certain goods, services, and personalities.

Food editors perform a wide range of functions, but their primary responsibility is to ensure that text provided by food writers is suitable in content, format, and style for the intended audiences.

Food writers and editors work for magazines, trade journals, newspapers, books, and radio and television broadcasts. They may also work as freelancers.

HISTORY

The skill of writing has existed for thousands of years; writing about food has probably existed just as long. Recipes have been found recorded on clay tablets from Mesopotamia dating back more than 3,800 years. One of the oldest surviving cookbooks, *De Re Coquinaria,* is a collection of recipes generally attributed to a Roman gourmet by the name of Marcus Apicius, who lived during the 1st century.

After many centuries of writing recipes and cookbooks, people moved on to writing about food, its preparation, and reviewing food-serving establishments. One of the first magazines in the United States

QUICK FACTS

School Subjects
English
Journalism

Personal Skills
Communication/ideas
Helping/teaching

Work Environment
Primarily indoors
Primarily one location

Minimum Education Level
Bachelor's degree

Salary Range
$22,090 to $42,330 to
    $87,390+ (writers)
$24,590 to $41,460 to
    $80,000+ (editors)

Certification or Licensing
None available

Outlook
About as fast as the average

DOT
131, 132

GOE
01.01.01, 01.01.02

NOC
5121, 5122

O*NET-SOC
27-3041.00, 27-3043.00

dedicated solely to food and wine, *Gourmet,* was published in 1941. *Gourmet* was also the first U.S. magazine to regularly publish restaurant reviews, something that is quite common now.

Today, there are many magazines devoted to food, and most newspapers have sections devoted to food, as well. Take a walk down the food/cookbook aisle at any bookstore and the sheer number of books and the variety of food topics covered may amaze you. Today, food writers and editors are busier than ever.

THE JOB

Food writers and editors deal with the written word, whether the completed work is the printed page, broadcast, or computer screen. The nature of their work is as varied as the materials they produce: magazines, newspapers, books, trade journals and other publications, advertisements, and scripts for radio and television broadcast. The one common factor is the subject: food.

Food writers need to be able to write very descriptively, since the reader will not be able to taste, touch, or smell the product they are writing about. Depending on whether or not pictures accompany the written word, the reader may not even be able to see it. Food writers use their writing skills to write about many different things. They might write a press release about a new food product to be distributed to food editors at numerous newspapers and magazines. They may write a story about seasonal fruits and vegetables for a local television news broadcast. They may write an article for a women's magazine about new cooking utensils that make meal preparation easier for amateur chefs. They may write a review about the new restaurant that just opened.

Food writers who work for newspapers or magazines generally write about all things related to food and beverages, such as recipes, new food products, meal planning and preparation, grocery shopping, cooking utensils and related products, and establishments that serve food and beverages. Some food writers also cover other subject areas, as well, especially if they work for a newspaper or a general interest magazine, as opposed to a magazine dedicated solely to food.

Perhaps the most infamous type of food writer is the food/restaurant critic. The critic needs to be objective and fair with any type of product or restaurant review. When dining at a restaurant, he or she also needs to be anonymous, which is not always easy. While dining, food/restaurant critics need to make accurate observations and try to write or record them without arousing the suspicion of the restaurant staff, lest they realize they are being reviewed.

Food editors need to be able to polish the work of a food writer into a finished article or book. They correct grammar, spelling, and style, and check all the facts, especially where recipes are concerned. They are responsible for making sure that the writing adheres to any pertinent style guidelines, and that the writing is appropriate for the intended audience. When working for a magazine or newspaper, food editors may also be responsible for planning the editorial content of an entire food section, which can range in size from as little as half of a page to a multiple-page spread. Their duties may include assigning stories to staff or freelance writers, as well as assigning photography or artwork assignments as needed, to accompany the articles and recipes.

Food writers and editors who work for publishing houses may work on tour or guidebooks, writing and editing restaurant reviews and stories about regional food specialties. Or they may work with recipes and cookbooks, meticulously checking to ensure all ingredients and measurements are correct, and that no steps have been omitted from the cooking directions.

Food writers and editors can be employed either as in-house staff or as freelancers. Freelancers must provide their own office space and equipment, such as computers and fax machines. Freelance writers also are responsible for keeping tax records, sending out invoices, negotiating contracts, and providing their own health insurance.

REQUIREMENTS
High School
If you are interested in becoming a food writer or an editor, take English, general science, home economics, and computer classes while in high school. If they are offered at your school, take elective classes in writing or editing, such as journalism and business communications. Editors and writers in any areas must be expert communicators, so you should excel in English. You must learn to write well, since you will be correcting and even rewriting the work of others. While in high school, participating with the school's newspaper, yearbook, or any other publication will be of benefit to you.

Postsecondary Training
Most food writing and editing jobs require a college education. Some employers desire communications or journalism training in college. Others will require culinary coursework. Most schools offer courses in journalism and some have more specialized courses in

book publishing, publication management, and newspaper and magazine writing.

Some employers require a degree or certificate from culinary school, or culinary work experience, in addition to a background in writing or editing. You may wish to take cooking classes from a local culinary school or community college to enhance your marketability as a food writer or editor.

In addition to formal course work, most employers look for practical writing and editing experience of any kind. Experience with college newspapers, yearbooks, or literary magazines will give you an edge, as well as if you have worked for small community newspapers or radio stations, even in an unpaid position. Many businesses, book publishers, magazines, newspapers, and radio and television stations have summer internship programs that provide valuable training. Interns do many simple tasks, such as running errands and answering phones, but some may be asked to perform research, conduct interviews, or even write or edit some minor pieces.

Other Requirements

In general, food writers and editors should be creative and able to express ideas clearly. Other assets include curiosity, persistence, initiative, resourcefulness, an accurate memory, and the ability to concentrate and produce quality work under pressure.

One last requirement, perhaps the most obvious, is that you should love food and everything to do with food. As a food writer or editor, you will spend much of your time sampling products, trying recipes, and writing or editing countless numbers of stories about food, so if you're not passionate about the subject, you will not be happy with your job.

EXPLORING

As a high school or college student, explore your interest in the fields of writing and editing by working as a reporter or writer on school newspapers, yearbooks, and literary magazines. If you cannot work for the school paper, try to land a part-time job on a local newspaper or newsletter. Explore your passion for food and increase your knowledge by taking cooking classes, attending ethnic festivals and food events, or touring different food-related businesses. Experiment with different types of restaurants and cuisines. After dining at a new restaurant, write about the experience. Review your writing. It is objective? Descriptive? Informative? Edit and rewrite it until you are satisfied with it.

Small community newspapers and local radio stations often welcome contributions from outside sources, although they may not be able to pay for them. Jobs in bookstores, magazine shops, and even newsstands offer a chance to become familiar with the various publications.

Professional organizations dedicated to food writing and editing, such as those listed at the end of this article, often provide information, resources, conferences, and other guidance programs that may be of interest to you.

EMPLOYERS

Food writers and editors work for a variety of employers. Magazines, newspapers, online publications, television and radio stations, book publishers, food/beverage manufacturing companies, and food/beverage trade associations all hire food writers and editors. Many food writers and editors work on a freelance basis, as well. Most employers are found in large cities such as New York, but virtually any geographical area served by a large newspaper will offer opportunities for a food writer or editor.

STARTING OUT

Most food writers and editors start out in entry-level positions. These jobs may be listed with college placement offices, or they may be obtained by applying directly to the employment departments of the individual newspapers, magazines, book publishers, or broadcasting companies. Graduates who previously had internships with these companies often have the advantage of knowing someone who can give them a personal recommendation or inform them of potential job openings before they are made public, thus giving them an edge over the competition. Want ads in newspapers and trade journals or on websites of professional associations are another source for jobs.

Some food writers and editors may start out writing and editing in a different subject area, and later choose to work with food when they have more seniority and priority in choosing work assignments. Other food writers and editors gain experience by freelancing, one article or review at a time. Even unpaid assignments can benefit the aspiring food writer or editor. They allow you to build up your portfolio of food-related writing and editing samples and provide you with contact with the people who may be in a position to hire you at a later time.

ADVANCEMENT

Food writers and editors are usually rewarded with higher profile assignments and increase in salary as they gain experience. For example, food writers may advance by moving from writing short filler copy or covering local events, to writing main features or traveling to cover high-profile industry events. In many cases, food writers and editors advance by moving from a position on one publication to the same position with a larger or more prestigious publication. Such moves may bring significant increases in both pay and status.

Sometimes freelance food writers and editors accept full-time positions with a newspaper or magazine. Such positions are usually offered on the merit of their previous freelance work for a publication. Other freelance food writers and editors may prefer to remain freelancers, but are able to command a higher paycheck because of their reputation and experience.

EARNINGS

In 2003, the median salary for writers, including food writers, was $42,330 a year, according to the U.S. Department of Labor (USDL). The lowest paid 10 percent earned less than $22,090, while the highest paid 10 percent earned $87,390 or more.

The USDL reports that the median annual salary for editors, including food editors, was $41,460 in 2003. The lowest paid 10 percent earned $24,590 or less, while the highest paid 10 percent earned $77,430 or more.

The International Association of Culinary Professionals (IACP) compiled a list of median salaries in 2002 for careers in the culinary field, including the following: cookbook author, $5,000 to $10,000 on their first book; cookbook editor, $27,000 to $85,000 annually; magazine food editor, $41,000 to $80,000 annually; newspaper food editor, $39,000 to $61,000 annually; food writer on staff at a publication, $19,000 to $40,000 annually; freelance food writer, $100 to $1,000 per story. In general, salaries are higher in large cities. Salaries are also dependent on the employer, as larger publications tend to pay more, and the writer or editor's level of experience, as those with many years of experience are able to earn a larger salary.

In addition to their salaries, many food writers and editors receive additional compensation. Most food critics, for example, have the meals they eat at a restaurant for the purpose of a review paid for by their employer. Some food writers and editors also receive travel expenses to cover expenditures such as mileage from driving to cover local events, or airfare and hotel accommodations for covering out-of-town industry events.

WORK ENVIRONMENT

Working conditions vary for food writers. Although the workweek usually runs 35 to 40 hours, many writers work during non-traditional hours or work overtime. Writers often work nights and weekends to cover food and beverage industry events, review restaurants, or to meet deadlines.

Many food writers work independently, but they often must cooperate with artists, photographers, editors, or advertising people who may have differing opinions of how the materials should be prepared and presented.

Physical surroundings range from comfortable private offices to noisy, crowded newsrooms filled with other workers typing and talking on the telephone. Food writers may be able to do much research via the library, Internet, or telephone interviews, but often may travel to local sites, other cities, or even out of the country.

The environments in which food editors work vary widely. Most editors work in private offices or cubicles. Book and magazine food editors often work in quieter surroundings than do newspaper food editors, who sometimes work in rather loud and hectic situations.

As with food writers, virtually all food editors must deal with the demands of deadlines. Newspaper and magazine food editors work in a much more pressurized atmosphere than book food editors because they face daily or weekly deadlines, whereas book production usually takes place over several months. In almost all cases, though, food editors must work long hours during certain phases of the editing process.

OUTLOOK

The employment of writers and editors, including food writers and editors, is expected to increase about as fast as the average rate of all occupations through 2012, according to the *Occupational Outlook Handbook*.

Individuals entering this field should realize that the competition for jobs is intense. Students just out of college may especially have difficulty finding employment. However, the subject of food and beverages continues to grow in popularity, thus providing more opportunities for those who wish to pursue a career in food writing and editing.

FOR MORE INFORMATION

The following organization is an excellent source of information about careers in copyediting. The ACES organizes educational seminars and maintains lists of internships.
American Copy Editors Society (ACES)
3 Healy Street
Huntington, NY 11743
http://www.copydesk.org

The Fund provides information about internships and about the newspaper business in general.
Dow Jones Newspaper Fund
PO Box 300
Princeton, NJ 08543-0300
Tel: 609-452-2820
Email: newsfund@wsj.dowjones.com
http://djnewspaperfund.dowjones.com/fund

The following is an organization for freelance editors. Members receive a newsletter and a free listing in their directory.
Editorial Freelancers Association (EFA)
71 West 23rd Street, Suite 1910
New York, NY 10010-4102
Tel: 866-929-5400
Email: info@the-efa.org
http://www.the-efa.org

This organization provides a wealth of industry information at its website.
International Association of Culinary Professionals
304 West Liberty Street, Suite 201
Louisville, KY 40202
Tel: 502-581-9786
Email: iacp@hqtrs.com
http://www.iacp.com

This organization offers student membership, and an online newsletter and magazine at its website.
International Food, Wine & Travel Writers Association
1142 South Diamond Bar Boulevard, #177
Diamond Bar, CA 91765-2203
Tel: 877-439-8929
http://www.ifwtwa.org

The following organization is a good source of information about internships:

Magazine Publishers of America
810 Seventh Avenue, 24th Floor
New York, NY 10019
Email: mpa@magazine.org
http://www.magazine.org

This organization offers student memberships for those interested in opinion writing.

National Conference of Editorial Writers
3899 North Front Street
Harrisburg, PA 17110
Tel: 717-703-3015
Email: ncew@pa-news.org
http://www.ncew.org

The following organization's website provides information on issues facing food writers and editors, such as ethics, spelling guidelines, and criticism guidelines.

Association of Food Journalists (AFJ)
http://www.afjonline.com

This website offers online courses and a newsletter on writing about food.

Food Writing
Email: editor@food-writing.com
http://www.food-writing.com

INTERVIEW

Nancy Ryan is a food writer and editor. She spoke with the editors of Careers in Focus: Journalism *about her career.*

Q. How long have you been a food writer/editor?

A. I have been writing about food for 30 years. During that time I was a food editor for a magazine for 15 years, then opened my own freelance food writing biz, then took my most recent job as culinary editor for *Plate*, a national magazine for chefs and restaurateurs two-and-a-half years ago. I also develop recipes, and have edited/written three cookbooks and am at work on another.

Q. What are the features of a well-written article about food?

A. First, good writing. By that, I mean grammatical, well-constructed prose with a "voice" or persona behind it and a great lead sentence or paragraph. Otherwise, why read it? Second, and equally important, a broad base of food knowledge and impeccable research about the topic/subject of the article.

Q. How did you train for this job?

A. I was a foodie all my life; my parents were foodies. I received a degree in journalism, and then got a newspaper job right out of college. I started my career writing on the society pages of the former *Times Herald* newspaper in Washington, D.C. My penchant for food eventually landed me in the food department.

Q. What are the most important professional qualities for food writers/editors?

A. • excellent writing skills
  • a style or voice
  • broad knowledge of food, food history, and ongoing self-education
  • impeccable research ability
  • experience working in a restaurant during some part of their career for training

Q. What are some of the pros and cons of your job?

A. Pros: Food writing and editing is the most interesting job in the world.

Cons: This career can lead to weight gain. And by working at home, you can theoretically work 24 hours a day, seven days a week. Whether you work from a home office or the office of your employer, this career makes it hard to structure time efficiently, and it is easy to become a workaholic. In addition to writing and researching, there are endless restaurant openings and events to attend.

Q. In your experience, what type of companies or organizations employ food writers/editors?

A. Book publishers hire editors with food expertise to edit cookbooks and also be acquisition editors—to find cookbook projects. This requires a great deal of experience. In addition, magazines and newspapers hire full- and part-time food writers and freelance food writers. Restaurant reviewing—for magazines and newspapers—is another avenue for food writers.

Q. What advice would you give high school students who are interested in becoming food writers/editors?

A. Read, read, read about food and the writing of other food writers whom you admire. Work in a restaurant. You will start at the bottom, but the hands-on learning can't be duplicated. A culinary degree is a good thing! It only takes two years. Barring that, take some cooking classes. Learn how to write well and polish your skills constantly.

Foreign Correspondents

QUICK FACTS

School Subjects
English
Foreign language
Journalism

Personal Skills
Communication/ideas
Helping/teaching

Work Environment
Indoors and outdoors
Primarily multiple locations

Minimum Education Level
Bachelor's degree

Salary Range
$17,900 to $50,000 to
$100,000

Certification or Licensing
None available

Outlook
Little or no change

DOT
N/A

GOE
N/A

NOC
5123

O*NET-SOC
27-3022.00

OVERVIEW

Foreign correspondents report on news from countries outside of where their newspapers, radio or television networks, or wire services are located. They sometimes work for a particular newspaper, but since today's media are more interested in local and national news, they usually rely on reports from news wire services to handle international news coverage rather than dispatching their own reporters to the scene. Only the biggest newspapers and television networks employ foreign correspondents. These reporters are usually stationed in a particular city and cover a wide territory.

HISTORY

James Gordon Bennett Sr., a prominent United States journalist and publisher of the *New York Herald*, was responsible for many firsts in the newspaper industry. He was the first publisher to sell papers through newsboys, the first to use illustrations for news stories, the first to publish stock-market prices and daily financial articles, and he was the first to employ European correspondents. Bennett's son, James Gordon Bennett Jr., carried on the family business and in 1871 sent Henry M. Stanley to central Africa to find Dr. David Livingstone, a famous British explorer who had disappeared.

In the early days, even magazines employed foreign correspondents. Famous American poet Ezra Pound, for example, reported from London for *Poetry* and *The Little Review*.

The inventions of the telegraph, telephone, typewriter, portable typewriter, the portable laptop computer, and the Internet all have contributed to the growth of foreign correspondence.

THE JOB

The foreign correspondent is stationed in a foreign country where his or her job is to report on the news there. Foreign news can range from the violent (wars, coups, and refugee situations) to the calm (cultural events and financial issues). Although a domestic correspondent is responsible for covering specific areas of the news, like politics, health, sports, consumer affairs, business, or religion, foreign correspondents are responsible for all of these areas in the country where they are stationed. A China-based correspondent, for example, could spend a day covering the new trade policy between the United States and China, and the next day report on the religious persecution of Christians by the Chinese government.

A foreign correspondent often is responsible for more than one country. Depending on where he or she is stationed, the foreign correspondent might have to act as a one-person band in gathering and preparing stories.

"There are times when the phone rings at five in the morning and you're told to go to Pakistan," said Michael Lev, Beijing, China, correspondent for the *Chicago Tribune*. "You must keep your wits about you and figure out what to do next."

For the most part, Lev decides on his own story ideas, choosing which ones interest him the most out of a myriad of possibilities. But foreign correspondents alone are responsible for getting the story done, and unlike reporters back home, they have little or no support staff to help them. Broadcast foreign correspondents, for example, may have to do their own audio editing after filming scenes. And just like other news reporters, foreign correspondents work under the pressure of deadlines. In addition, they often are thrown into unfamiliar situations in strange places.

Part of the importance of a foreign correspondent's job is keeping readers or viewers aware of the various cultures and practices held by the rest of the world. Lev says he tries to focus on similarities and differences between the Asian countries he covers and the United States. "If you don't understand another culture, you are more likely to come into conflict with it," he says.

Foreign correspondents are drawn to conflicts of all kinds, especially war. They may choose to go to the front of a battle to get an

Did You Know?

- More than 54 million newspapers are sold daily in the United States.
- Nearly 80 percent of adults in the top 50 U.S. markets read a newspaper each week.
- More than 1,500 newspapers have a presence on the Web. Visit http://www.newsvoyager.com/voyager.cfm to access many of these publications.
- Approximately 381,000 people were employed in the U.S. newspaper industry in 2003.
- More than 73 percent (or 9 million tons) of newspapers in the United States were recycled in 2003.

Source: Facts About Newspapers 2004

accurate picture of what's happening. Or they may be able to get the story from a safer position. Sometimes they face weapons trained directly on them.

Much of a foreign correspondent's time is spent doing research, investigating leads, setting up appointments, making travel arrangements, making on-site observations, and interviewing local people or those involved in the situation. The foreign correspondent often must be experienced in taking photographs or shooting video.

Living conditions can be rough or primitive, sometimes with no running water. The job can sometimes be isolating.

After correspondents have interviewed sources and noted observations about an event or filmed it, they put their stories together, writing on computers and using modern technology like the Internet, email, satellite telephones, and fax machines to finish the job and transmit the story to their newspaper, broadcast station, or wire service. Many times, correspondents work out of hotel rooms.

REQUIREMENTS

High School

In addition to English and creative writing needed for a career in journalism, you should study languages, social studies, political science, history, and geography. Initial experience may be gained by working on your school newspaper or yearbook, or taking advantage of study-abroad programs.

Postsecondary Training
In college, pursuing a journalism major is helpful but may not be crucial to obtaining a job as a foreign correspondent. Classes, or even a major, in history, political science, or literature could be beneficial. Study in economics and foreign languages are also helpful.

Other Requirements
To be a foreign correspondent, in addition to a definite love of adventure, you need to be curious about how other people live, diplomatic when interviewing people, have the courage to sometimes confront people on uncomfortable topics, the ability to communicate well, and the discipline to sometimes act as your own boss. You also need to be strong enough to hold up under pressure yet flexible enough to adapt to other cultures.

EXPLORING

Does this type of work interest you? To explore this field, you can begin by honing your skills in different journalism media. Join your high school newspaper staff to become a regular columnist or write special feature articles. Check out your high school's TV station, if it has one, and audition to be an anchor. If your school has a radio station, volunteer to be on the staff there. If your school has a student-maintained website, get involved with that project. Gain as much experience as you can using different media to learn about the strengths and weaknesses of each and find out where you fit in best. You can also ask your high school journalism teacher or guidance counselor to help you set up an informational interview with a local journalist. Most are happy to speak with you when they know you are interested in their careers. It may be possible to get a part-time or summer job working at a local TV or radio station or at the newspaper office. Competition for one of these jobs, however, is strong because many college students take such positions as interns and do the work for little or no pay.

EMPLOYERS

Foreign correspondents work for news wire services, such as the Associated Press, United Press International, Reuters, and Agence-France Press; major metropolitan newspapers; news magazines; and television and radio networks. These media are located in the largest cities in the United States and in the case of Reuters and Agence-France Press, in Europe.

STARTING OUT

College graduates have a couple of paths to choose between to become a foreign correspondent. They can decide to experience what being a foreign correspondent is like immediately by going to another country, perhaps one whose language is familiar to them, and freelancing or working as a *stringer*. That means writing stories and offering them to anyone who will buy them. This method can be hard to accomplish financially in the short run but can pay off substantially in the long run.

Another path is to take the traditional route of a journalist and try to get hired upon graduation at any newspaper, radio station, or television station you can. It helps in this regard to have worked at a summer internship during your college years. Recent college graduates generally get hired at small newspapers or media stations, although a few major metropolitan dailies will employ top graduates for a year with no guarantee of their being kept on afterward. After building experience at a small paper or station, a reporter can try to find work at progressively bigger ones. Reporters who find employment at a major metropolitan daily that uses foreign correspondents can work their way through the ranks to become one. This is the path Michael Lev took, and he became a foreign correspondent when he was in his early 30s. He suggests that working for a wire service may allow a reporter to get abroad faster, but he thinks more freedom can be found working for a newspaper.

ADVANCEMENT

Foreign correspondents can advance to other locations that are more appealing to them or that offer a bigger challenge. Or they can return home to become columnists, editorial writers, editors, or network news directors.

EARNINGS

Salaries vary greatly depending on the publication, network, or station, and the cost of living and tax structure in various places around the world where foreign correspondents work. Generally, salaries range from $50,000 to an average of about $75,000 to a peak of $100,000 or more. Some media will pay for living expenses, such as the costs of a home, school for the reporter's children, and a car.

According to the U.S. Department of Labor, correspondents and other news reporters earned a median salary of $31,240 in 2003. The lowest 10 percent earned $17,900 or less, and the highest 10 percent earned $71,520 or more.

WORK ENVIRONMENT

Correspondents and other reporters may face a hectic work environment if they have tight deadlines and have to produce their reports with little time for preparation. Correspondents who work in countries that face great political or social problems risk their health and even their lives to report breaking news. Covering wars, political uprisings, fires, floods, and similar events can be extremely dangerous.

Working hours vary depending on the correspondent's deadlines. Their work often demands irregular or long hours. Because foreign correspondents report from international locations, this job involves travel. The amount of travel depends on the size of the region the correspondent covers.

OUTLOOK

Although employment at newspapers, radio stations, and television stations in general is expected to continue to decline, the number of foreign correspondent jobs has leveled off. The employment outlook is expected to remain relatively stable.

Factors that keep the number of foreign correspondents low are the high cost of maintaining a foreign news bureau and the relative lack of interest Americans show in world news. Despite these factors, the number of correspondents is not expected to decrease. There are simply too few as it is; decreasing the number could put the job in danger of disappearing, which most journalists believe is not an option. For now and the near future, most job openings will arise from the need to replace those correspondents who leave the job.

FOR MORE INFORMATION

For a list of accredited programs in journalism and mass communications, visit the ACEJMC website.
    Accrediting Council on Education in Journalism and Mass
        Communications (ACEJMC)
    University of Kansas School of Journalism
        and Mass Communications
    Stauffer-Flint Hall, 1435 Jayhawk Boulevard
    Lawrence, KS 66045-7575
    http://www.ku.edu/~acejmc/STUDENT/PROGLIST.SHTML

The ASJA promotes the interests of freelance writers. It provides information on court rulings dealing with writing issues, has a writers' referral service, and offers a newsletter.

American Society of Journalists and Authors (ASJA)
1501 Broadway, Suite 302
New York, NY 10036
Tel: 212-997-0947
http://www.asja.org

This association provides the annual publication Journalism and Mass Communication Directory *with information on educational programs in all areas of journalism (newspapers, magazines, television, and radio).*

Association for Education in Journalism and Mass Communication
234 Outlet Pointe Boulevard
Columbia, SC 29210-5667
Tel: 803-798-0271
Email: aejmc@aejmc.org
http://www.aejmc.org

Founded in 1958 by the Wall Street Journal *to improve the quality of journalism education, this organization offers internships, scholarships, and literature for college students. To read* The Journalist's Road to Success: A Career Guide, *which lists schools offering degrees in news-editing, and financial aid to those interested in print journalism, visit the DJNF website:*

Dow Jones Newspaper Fund (DJNF)
PO Box 300
Princeton, NJ 08543-0300
Tel: 609-452-2820
Email: newsfund@wsj.dowjones.com
http://djnewspaperfund.dowjones.com/fund

The NAB website's Career Center has information on jobs, scholarships, internships, college programs, and other resources. You can also purchase career publications from the online NAB Store.

National Association of Broadcasters (NAB)
1771 N Street, NW
Washington, DC 20036
Tel: 202-429-5300
Email: nab@nab.org
http://www.nab.org

The SPJ has chapters all over the United States. The SPJ website offers career information and information on internships and fellowships.
Society of Professional Journalists (SPJ)
Eugene S. Pulliam National Journalism Center
3909 North Meridian Street
Indianapolis, IN 46208
Tel: 317-927-8000
Email: questions@spj.org
http://spj.org

Visit the following website for comprehensive information on journalism careers, summer programs, and college journalism programs.
High School Journalism
http://www.highschooljournalism.org

For comprehensive information for citizens, students, and news people about the field of journalism, visit
Project for Excellence in Journalism and the Committee of
Concerned Journalists
http://www.journalism.org

Illustrators

QUICK FACTS

School Subjects
Art
Computer science
Journalism

Personal Skills
Artistic
Following instructions

Work Environment
Primarily indoors
Primarily one location

Minimum Education Level
High school diploma

Salary Range
$17,160 to $55,840 to
$74,080+

Certification or Licensing
Voluntary

Outlook
About as fast as the average

DOT
141

GOE
01.04.01

NOC
5241

O*NET-SOC
27-1013.01

OVERVIEW

Illustrators prepare charts, graphs, maps, and other drawings for newspapers, magazines, books, advertisements, packaging, websites, computer programs, and other formats.

HISTORY

The history of illustration can be traced back to the 8th century. Several famous illuminated manuscripts were created in the Middle Ages, including the *Book of Kells*. In the 15th century, movable type was introduced and came to be used by book illustrators. Other printing methods such as etching, woodcuts, and copper engravings were used as illustration techniques in the 16th century and beyond.

In 1796, lithography was invented in Germany. In the original process of lithography, artists made prints directly from designs drawn on slabs of stone. Metal sheets eventually replaced these stone slabs. By the mid-1800s, illustrators used lithographs and engravings to draw magazine and newspaper pages.

As knowledge of photography developed and advanced reproduction processes were invented, artists increasingly used photographs as illustrations. Many industries today, ranging from journalism to advertising to fashion, employ illustrators.

THE JOB

Illustrators create print and electronic illustrations for newspapers, magazines, and books. These illustrations are used to describe, inform, clarify, instruct, decorate, and draw attention. Examples of illustrations that appear in these publications include a colorful chart at a newspaper's website that compares the views of two political candidates, a bar graph in *USA Today* made out of dollar signs that conveys rising home prices over the past decade, a map that details national parks in a newspaper's travel section, a stylized drawing of Britney Spears to illustrate a story about the pop star in *Rolling Stone,* and any other type of illustration that helps readers to more easily understand a story.

Illustrators use a variety of media for their work—pencil, pen and ink, pastels, paints (oil, acrylic, and watercolor), airbrush, collage, and computer technology. In addition to creating illustrations for newspaper, magazine, and book publishers, their work appears in advertisements, signs and billboards, packaging (for everything from milk cartons to CDs), websites, computer programs, greeting cards, calendars, stationery, and direct mail.

Illustrators often work as part of a creative team, which can include graphic designers, photographers, art directors, Web designers, writers, and editors.

Two of the fastest growing specialties in illustration are fashion illustration and medical illustration.

Fashion illustrators work in a glamorized, intense environment. Their artistic focus is specifically on styles of clothing and personal image. Illustrators can work in a few different categories of the fashion field. They provide artwork to accompany editorial pieces in magazines such as *Glamour, Redbook*, and *Vogue,* and newspapers such as *Women's Wear Daily.* They may also be employed by catalog companies and fashion designers.

Medical illustrators use graphics and drawings to make medical concepts and descriptions easier to understand. Medical illustrators provide illustrations of anatomical and biological structures and processes, as well as surgical and medical techniques and procedures. Their work is found in the health sections of newspapers, medical magazines and journals, textbooks, advertisements for medical products, instructional films and videotapes, television programs, exhibits, lectures and presentations, and computer-assisted learning programs. A medical illustrator may work in a wide range of medical and biological areas or specialize in a particular area, such as cell structure, blood, disease, or the eye. Much of their work is done with computers; however, they must still have strong skills in traditional drawing and drafting techniques.

REQUIREMENTS
High School
In illustration, creative talent is more important than education. However, there are academic programs in illustration at most colleges and universities. If you are considering going on to a formal program, be sure to take plenty of art classes while in high school. Elective classes in illustration, ceramics, painting, or photography are common courses offered at many high schools.

Postsecondary Training
To find a salaried position as a general illustrator, you should have at least a high school diploma and preferably an associate or bachelor's degree in commercial art or fine art. Whether you are looking for full-time employment or freelance assignments, you will need an organized collection of samples of your best work, which is called a portfolio. Employers are especially interested in work that has been published or printed. An advantage to pursuing education beyond high school is that it gives you an opportunity to build your portfolio.

Fashion illustrators should study clothing construction, fashion design, and cosmetology in addition to taking art courses. They should also keep up with the latest fashion and illustration trends by reading fashion magazines.

Medical illustrators are required to earn a bachelor's degree in either biology or art and then complete an advanced degree program in medical illustration.

Certification or Licensing
Illustrators need to continue their education and training while pursuing their careers. Licensing and certification are not required for general illustrators. However, illustrators must keep up with the latest innovations in design techniques, computer software, and presentation technology, as well as technological advances in the fields for which they provide illustrations.

Most medical illustrators are members of the Association of Medical Illustrators (AMI). The AMI offers voluntary certification in medical illustration to its members.

Other Requirements
Illustrators must be creative, and, of course, demonstrate artistic talent and skill. They also need to be flexible. Because their art is often commercial in nature, illustrators must be willing to accommodate their employers' desires if they are to build a broad clientele and earn

a decent living. They must be able to take suggestions and rejections gracefully.

EXPLORING

You can explore an interest in this career by taking art courses. Artists can always improve their drawing skills by practicing on their own, either producing original artwork, or making sketches from drawings that appear in textbooks and reference manuals that relate to their interests. Participation in art, fashion, and science clubs is also good exposure. You might also work as an illustrator on your school newspaper or other publications.

EMPLOYERS

More than half of all visual artists are self-employed. Illustrators can find employment at newspapers, magazines, and other publishers throughout the United States. Illustrators who do not work in journalism can find employment at advertising agencies, design firms, commercial art and reproduction firms, and printing and publishing firms. They can also find employment in the motion picture and television industries, wholesale and retail trade establishments, and public relations firms.

Medical illustrators are employed at medical and scientific publishers, hospitals, medical centers, schools, laboratories, pharmaceutical companies, and advertising agencies. Fashion illustrators are employed at magazines, newspapers, and catalog companies.

STARTING OUT

Graduates of illustration programs should develop a portfolio of their work to show to prospective newspaper or magazine publishers. Most schools offer career counseling and job placement assistance to their graduates. Job ads and employment agencies are also potential sources for locating work.

Medical illustrators can also find job placement assistance with the AMI. In addition to the job leads, AMI also provides certification that is often preferred by employers.

ADVANCEMENT

After an illustrator gains experience, he or she will be given more challenging and unusual work. They might move from a small, local newspaper to a national newspaper such as *USA Today*. Those with strong computer skills will have the best chances for advancement. Illustrators can advance by developing skills in a specialized area, or even starting their own business. Illustrators can also go into teaching in colleges and universities at the undergraduate and graduate levels.

EARNINGS

The pay for illustrations can be as little as receiving a byline, though in the beginning of your career it may be worth it just to get exposure. Some illustrators can earn several thousand dollars for a single illustration. Freelance work is often uncertain because of the fluctuation in pay rates and steadiness of work. The U.S. Department of Labor reports that median earnings for salaried fine artists, including painters, sculptors, and illustrators, were $35,420 a year in 2003. The top 10 percent earned more than $74,080 and the bottom 10 percent earned less than $17,160. Fine artists employed by newspaper and book publishers had mean annual earnings of $55,840 in 2003.

Illustrators generally receive good benefits, including health and life insurance, pension plans, and vacation, sick, and holiday pay.

WORK ENVIRONMENT

Illustrators generally work in clean, well-lit newsrooms or offices. They spend a great deal of time at their desks, whether in front of a computer or at the drafting table. Medical illustrators are sometimes required to visit operating rooms and other health care settings. Fashion illustrators may be required to attend fashion shows and other industry events.

Illustrators must be able to deal with deadline pressure since newspapers and magazines are published daily, weekly, or monthly. Illustrators who produce content for news-related websites may have to create or replace existing online content frequently during a busy news day.

OUTLOOK

Employment of visual artists is expected to grow about as fast as the average for all occupations through 2012, according to the *Occupational Outlook Handbook*. The growth of the Internet should provide opportunities for illustrators, although the increased use of computer-aided design systems is a threat because individuals do not necessarily need artistic talent or training to use them.

The outlook for careers in fashion illustration is dependent on the growth of the magazine and newspaper publishing industries. The popularity of American fashion in other parts of the world will also create a demand for fashion illustrators to provide the artwork needed to sell to a global market.

The employment outlook for medical illustrators is very good. Because there are only a few graduate programs in medical illustration with small graduation classes, medical illustrators will find great demand for their skills. The field of medicine and science in general is always growing, and medical illustrators will be needed to depict new techniques, procedures, and discoveries in medical and science publications.

FOR MORE INFORMATION

For more information about careers in graphic design, contact
American Institute of Graphic Arts
164 Fifth Avenue
New York, NY 10010
Tel: 212-807-1990
Email: comments@aiga.org
http://www.aiga.org

For information on educational and career opportunities for medical illustrators, contact
Association of Medical Illustrators
245 First Street
Cambridge, MA 02142
Tel: 617-395-8186
Email: hq@ami.org
http://medical-illustrators.org

For information on the newspaper industry, contact
Dow Jones Newspaper Fund (DJNF)
PO Box 300
Princeton, NJ 08543-0300
Tel: 609-452-2820
Email: newsfund@wsj.dowjones.com
http://djnewspaperfund.dowjones.com/fund

This organization is committed to improving conditions for all creators of graphic art and to raising standards for the entire industry. For information, contact

Graphic Artists Guild
90 John Street, Suite 403
New York, NY 10038-3202
Tel: 212-791-3400
http://www.gag.org

For industry statistics, information on diversity, and to view a PowerPoint presentation entitled "Tips on Finding a Job in Magazines" visit the MPA website.

Magazine Publishers of America (MPA)
810 Seventh Avenue, 24th Floor
New York, NY 10019
Email: mpa@magazine.org
http://www.magazine.org

For information on education programs, contact

National Association of Schools of Art and Design
11250 Roger Bacon Drive, Suite 21
Reston, VA 20190-5248
Tel: 703-437-0700
Email: info@arts-accredit.org
http://nasad.arts-accredit.org

This national institution promotes and stimulates interest in the art of illustration by offering exhibits, lectures, educational programs, and social exchange. For information, contact

Society of Illustrators
128 East 63rd Street
New York, NY 10021-7303
Tel: 212-838-2560
Email: si1901@aol.com
http://www.societyillustrators.org

Journalism Teachers

OVERVIEW

Journalism teachers teach students the rudiments of journalistic writing. They develop teaching outlines and lesson plans, give lectures, facilitate discussions and activities, keep class attendance records, assign homework, and evaluate student progress. They teach at the secondary and postsecondary levels.

HISTORY

The first American newspaper, *Publick Occurrences Both Foreign and Domestick,* appeared in Boston in 1690, but lasted only one issue due to censorship by the British government. The first continuously published paper in America was the *Boston News-Letter,* first published in 1704. The first daily newspaper, the *Pennsylvania Evening Post,* began publication in 1783.

Despite a long tradition of newspaper journalism in the United States, it wasn't until 1869 that the first journalism course was offered at Washington College (now known as Washington and Lee University). In the following decades, a number of colleges and universities, most located in the Midwest, began offering journalism courses.

In 1903, Joseph Pulitzer, a newspaper magnate, gave Columbia University an endowment of $2 million to start a school of journalism. Despite the generous endowment, Columbia was unable to implement and start its new program until 1912. The first school of journalism in the United States—and the world—was founded in 1908 by Walter Williams, at the University of Missouri. Educators at the Missouri School of

QUICK FACTS

School Subjects
English
Journalism

Personal Skills
Communication/ideas
Helping/teaching

Work Environment
Primarily indoors
Primarily one location

Minimum Education Level
Bachelor's degree

Salary Range
$29,010 to $44,580 to $88,591+

Certification or Licensing
Voluntary (certification)
Required for certain positions (licensing)

Outlook
About as fast as the average (high school teachers)
Much faster than the average (college professors)

DOT
090

GOE
11.02.01

NOC
4121

O*NET-SOC
25-1122.00, 25-2031.00

A journalism teacher reviews
an assignment with a student.
(Photo Disc)

Journalism taught students using a hands-on approach in which they actually published a newspaper. (The school is still producing high-quality graduates today.)

In the early years of the 20th century, schools of journalism grew in popularity on our nation's campuses, and graduate journalism programs were introduced in the 1930s.

Today, journalism and communications programs (which often offer journalism majors) are extremely popular on our nation's campuses. The field of journalism has come a long way from its beginnings in the newspaper industry. The invention of radio, television, and the Internet have created countless opportunities for aspiring journalists, as well as the journalism teachers who prepare students for these careers.

THE JOB

High School Teachers

High school teachers who teach journalism may teach a variety of English courses, including journalism, or they may only teach journalism classes. Most high school journalism classes focus on the fundamentals of journalistic writing.

In the classroom, journalism teachers rely on a variety of teaching methods. They spend a great deal of time lecturing, but they also facilitate student discussion and develop projects and activities to interest the students in journalism. They make use of newspapers and other periodicals, show films and videos, use computers and the Internet, and bring in guest speakers. They assign writing exercises and other projects. Journalism teachers often require their students to spend some amount of time working on the school's newspaper or yearbook.

Outside of the classroom, journalism teachers prepare lectures, lesson plans, and exams. They evaluate student work and calculate grades. In the process of planning their class, journalism teachers read newspapers and magazines and monitor other new sources, such as television, radio, and the Internet to determine class assignments; photocopy notes, articles, and other handouts; and develop grading policies. They also continue to study alternative and traditional teaching methods to hone their skills. They prepare students for special events and conferences and submit student work to competitions. Journalism teachers also have the opportunity for extracurricular work as advisers to the school's publications, such as the newspaper or yearbook.

College Professors

Members of college and university faculty educate undergraduate or graduate students, or in some cases, both, in their areas of specialty. Journalism professors teach students about the fundamentals of journalistic writing, as well as more specialized topics such as investigative reporting, editorial writing, features writing, media criticism, and journalistic ethics. Some schools do not have a separate journalism department; many times journalism classes are taught under the auspices of the communications department.

The primary duty of a professor is his or her commitment to the students' education. Instruction takes place in the form of classroom lectures and in hands-on activities such as the actual publication of a newspaper, operation of a student-run television or radio station, or the creation of a news-based website. Textbooks usually supplement in-class learning, as do assignments, writing laboratories, exams, computers, local and national newspapers, and closed-circuit or cable television. Most professors teach three or four classes each week, totaling nine or 12 hours weekly. Much of a professor's time is spent preparing lectures and grading papers and exams, an additional two or three hours per class.

Journalism professors may also act as advisers for students. They set a certain amount of time aside to help students schedule a beneficial program of study, answer questions regarding their major, or any other aspects of college life. Not all professors serve as advisers; those who do may have a reduced teaching schedule to compensate.

Serving on department committees is another part of a professor's job. Topics such as academic or departmental issues, department budgets, equipment, new hires, or course curricula are often raised and discussed. Research and publishing both are very important responsibilities for professors. Publishing is a necessity to get and keep tenure-track positions. Tenure is a teaching status granted after a trial period that protects teachers from being fired without just cause. Professors who conduct research usually publish their findings in academic journals or books. In fact, many textbooks are written by college and university faculty.

REQUIREMENTS

High School
To prepare for a career as a journalism teacher—or, in fact, most any other kind of teacher—take a wide variety of college-preparatory classes, including science, history, computer science, English, and journalism. Prepare yourself to be comfortable speaking in front of people by taking speech classes or joining your school's speech or debate team

Postsecondary Training
If you want to be a journalism teacher, your college training will depend on the level at which you plan to teach. All 50 states and the District of Columbia require public high school teachers to have a bachelor's degree in either education or in the subject they teach. Prospective teachers must also complete an approved training program, which combines subject and educational classes with work experience in the classroom, called student teaching.

For prospective college or university professors, you will need at least one advanced degree in your chosen field of study. The master's degree is considered the minimum standard, and graduate work beyond the master's is usually desirable. If you hope to advance in academic rank above instructor, most institutions require a doctorate. Your graduate school program will be similar to a life of teaching—in addition to attending seminars, you'll research, prepare articles for publication, and teach some undergraduate courses.

Certification or Licensing
Journalism teachers and professors might consider becoming certified by the Journalism Education Association (see the end of this article

for contact information). Although it is not required, certification may boost an individual's attractiveness to employers during the job search.

High school teachers who work in public schools must be licensed under regulations established by the state in which they are teaching. If moving, teachers have to comply with any other regulations in their new state to be able to teach, though many states have reciprocity agreements that make it easier for teachers to change locations.

Licensure examinations test prospective teachers for competency in basic subjects such as mathematics, reading, writing, teaching, and other subject matter proficiency. In addition, many states are moving towards a performance-based evaluation for licensing. In this case, after passing the teaching examination, prospective teachers are given provisional licenses. Only after proving themselves capable in the classroom are they eligible for a full license.

Another growing trend spurred by recent teacher shortages in elementary and high schools is alternative licensure arrangements. For those who have a bachelor's degree but lack formal education courses and training in the classroom, states can issue a provisional license. These workers immediately begin teaching under the supervision of a licensed educator for one to two years and take education classes outside of their working hours. Once they have completed the required coursework and gained experience in the classroom, they are granted a full license.

College and university professors and high school teachers in private schools do not need to be licensed.

Other Requirements

Journalism teachers must respect their students as individuals, with personalities, strengths, and weaknesses of their own. They must also be patient and self-disciplined to manage a large group independently. Teachers should also be well organized, as you'll have to keep track of the work and progress of a number of different students.

If you aim to teach at the college level, you should enjoy reading, writing, and researching. Not only will you spend many years studying in school, but your whole career will be based on communicating your thoughts and ideas. People skills are important because you'll be dealing directly with students, administrators, and other faculty members on a daily basis. You should feel comfortable in a role of authority and possess self-confidence.

Where Do Teens Get Their News?

Not on the Internet, at least according to the *6th Annual Teen Report Card on Adults,* sponsored by the Uhlich Children's Advantage Network. The survey found that only 8.8 percent of teens surfed the Web for the latest news, while 56 percent reported that they boned up on current local, national, and international affairs via television. Newspapers (11.5 percent) came in a distant second to TV. So what are tech-savvy teenagers doing on the Internet? Emailing, instant messaging, and performing research.

EXPLORING

To explore a teaching career, look for leadership opportunities that involve working with children. You might find summer work as a counselor in a summer camp, as a leader of a scout troop, or as an assistant in a public park or community center. To get some firsthand teaching experience, volunteer for a tutoring program. To explore the area of journalism, join the newspaper or yearbook staff while in high school.

If you are interested in becoming a college professor, spend some time on a college campus to get a sense of the environment. Write to colleges or visit their websites to review their admissions brochures and course catalogs; read about the journalism or communications faculty members and the courses they teach. Before visiting college campuses, make arrangements to speak to journalism professors who teach courses that interest you. These professors may allow you to sit in on their classes and observe.

EMPLOYERS

There are more than 1.1 million secondary teachers employed in the United States. Journalism teachers make up a small percentage of this number. Although rural areas maintain schools, more teaching positions are available in urban or suburban areas. Journalism teachers are also finding opportunities in charter schools, which are smaller, deregulated schools that receive public funding.

There are nearly 20,500 postsecondary communications teachers (including journalism professors) employed in the United States. The majority of all college professors are employed in public and private four-year colleges and universities and two-year community colleges.

Employment opportunities vary based on area of study and education. With a doctorate, a number of publications, and a record of good teaching, journalism professors should find opportunities in universities all across the country.

STARTING OUT

While in college and graduate school, prospective journalism teachers should become familiar with their school's career services center to keep abreast of current teaching positions and journalism-related internships available. They should also consider joining associations such as the Journalism Education Association (JEA), Investigative Reporters and Editors (IRE), and the Society of Professional Journalists (SPJ). These organizations offer many resources, as well as provide informative meetings and conferences, which can also serve as great networking opportunities.

Prospective high school teachers can use their college career services offices and state departments of education to find job openings. Many local schools advertise teaching positions in newspapers. Another option is to directly contact the administration in the schools in which you'd like to work. While looking for a full-time position, you can work as a substitute teacher.

Prospective college professors should start the process of finding a teaching position while in graduate school. You will need to develop a curriculum vitae (a detailed academic resume), work on your academic writing, assist with research, attend conferences, and gain teaching experience and recommendations. Because of the competition for tenure-track positions, you may have to work for a few years in temporary positions. Some professional associations maintain lists of teaching opportunities in their areas. They may also make lists of applicants available to college administrators looking to fill an available position.

ADVANCEMENT

As high school journalism teachers acquire experience or additional education, they can expect higher wages and more responsibilities. Teachers with leadership skills and an interest in administrative work may advance to serve as principals or supervisors, though the number of these positions is limited and competition is fierce. In some high school systems, experienced teachers can become senior or mentor teachers. They help newer, less experienced teachers adjust to teaching, while continuing to maintain their own teaching duties. The additional responsibilities of serving as a mentor usually come with a higher rate of pay. Another move may be into higher education, teaching education classes at a college or university. For most of these positions, additional education is required.

At the college level, the normal pattern of advancement is from instructor to assistant professor, to associate professor, to full professor. All four academic ranks are concerned primarily with teaching and research. Some journalism teachers may choose to enter the administrative side of the field. A doctorate is not necessary, though helpful, at two-year colleges. It is an absolute necessity at four-year colleges and universities, as are service on departmental committees, research and publication, and a stellar teaching record. Some positions to consider are college president, dean, and departmental chairperson.

Some journalism teachers choose to leave the field for more lucrative careers in publishing or business. Many maintain a successful writing career running parallel to their teaching career.

EARNINGS

According to the U.S. Department of Labor, the median annual salary for high school teachers, including journalism teachers, was $44,580 in 2003. The lowest 10 percent earned less than $29,010, and the top 10 percent earned $69,710 or more. In general, private school teachers earn less than public school teachers.

High school journalism teachers can often earn additional pay by working with students in extracurricular activities, such as acting as an adviser to the school newspaper or yearbook; coaching sports; or teaching summer school. Other activities that can increase a teacher's salary include acting as a mentor to inexperienced teachers, or earning a master's degree or national certification.

College professors' earnings vary depending on their academic department, the size of the school, the type of school (public, private, women's only), and by the level of position the professor holds. According to the U.S. Department of Labor, the median annual salary for college and university communications teachers, including journalism teachers, was $49,030 in 2003. The lowest 10 percent earned $29,030, and the highest 10 percent earned $82,750 or more.

A 2003–04 salary survey by the American Association of University Professors found the average yearly income for all full-time university teachers was $66,475. It also reports that professors averaged the following salaries by rank: full professors, $88,591; associate professors, $63,063; assistant professors, $52,788; and instructors, $38,501.

College journalism professors often have additional earnings from activities such as research, writing for publication in scholarly journals, working in the field as a journalist, or other employment. In addition, many college and university full-time faculty members may have access to campus facilities, tuition waivers for dependents, housing and travel allowances, and paid sabbatical leaves. Part-time faculty members usually have fewer benefits.

WORK ENVIRONMENT

Most journalism teachers are contracted to work 10 months out of the year, with a two-month vacation during the summer. During their summer break, many continue their education to renew or upgrade their teaching licenses and earn higher salaries. Teachers in schools that operate year-round work eight-week sessions with one-week breaks in between and a five-week vacation in the winter.

High school journalism teachers work in generally pleasant conditions, although some older schools may have poor heating or electrical systems. The work can seem confining, requiring them to remain in the classroom throughout most of the day. Teachers may sometimes need to focus more on discipline issues with their students instead of actually teaching, which can be frustrating.

High school hours are generally 8:00 A.M. to 3:00 P.M., but journalism teachers work more than 40 hours a week teaching, preparing for classes, grading papers, and directing extracurricular activities. Similarly, most college journalism teachers work more than 40 hours each week, but their hours may vary. Many may teach classes in the evening or on the weekends. Although they may teach only two or three classes a semester, they spend many hours preparing for lectures, examining student work, and conducting research.

OUTLOOK

According to the *Occupational Outlook Handbook* (*OOH*), employment opportunities for high school teachers, including journalism teachers, are expected to grow as fast as the average for all occupations through 2012. The need to replace retiring teachers will provide many opportunities nationwide, but the demand will vary widely depending on geographic area. Inner-city schools characterized by poor working conditions and low salaries often suffer a shortage of teachers, as do remote, rural areas.

The *OOH* predicts much faster than average employment growth for college and university professors, including journalism professors, through 2012. College enrollment is projected to grow due to an increased number of 18- to 24-year-olds, an increased number of adults returning to college, and an increased number of foreign-born students, thus requiring the need for more college and university professors. Retirement of current faculty members will also provide job openings. However, it is predicted that many of the positions will be part time, and competition for full-time, tenure-track positions at four-year schools will be very strong.

FOR MORE INFORMATION

For information about careers, education, and union membership, contact the following organizations:

American Association of University Professors
1012 14th Street, NW, Suite 500
Washington, DC 20005
Tel: 202-737-5900
http://www.aaup.org

American Federation of Teachers
555 New Jersey Avenue, NW
Washington, DC 20001
Tel: 202-879-4400
Email: online@aft.org
http://www.aft.org

National Council for Accreditation of Teacher
   Education
2010 Massachusetts Avenue, NW, Suite 500
Washington, DC 20036
Tel: 202-466-7496
Email: ncate@ncate.org
http://www.ncate.org

National Education Association
1201 16th Street, NW
Washington, DC 20036-3290
Tel: 202-833-4000
http://www.nea.org

For information on investigative journalism and computer-assisted reporting, contact
Investigative Reporters and Editors
National Institute for Computer-Assisted Reporting
138 Neff Annex
Missouri School of Journalism
Columbia, MO 65211
Tel: 573-882-2042
Email: info@ire.org
http://www.ire.org

For information on journalism education, contact
Journalism Education Association
Kansas State University
103 Kedzie Hall
Manhattan, KS 66506-1505
Tel: 785-532-5532
http://www.jea.org

This organization for journalists has campus and online chapters.
Society of Professional Journalists (SPJ)
Eugene S. Pulliam National Journalism Center
3909 North Meridian Street
Indianapolis, IN 46208
Tel: 317-927-8000
http://www.spj.org

——— INTERVIEW ———

Rich Gordon is the Chair of the new media program at Northwestern University's Medill School of Journalism. He discussed the program and his career as a journalism professor with the editors of Careers in Focus: Journalism.

Q. Can you provide a brief overview of the Medill new media program?

A. Students interested in a master's degree in journalism at Medill have a choice of four sequences (academic programs): broadcast, magazine, reporting and writing, and new media. For most students it is a 12-month curriculum (four academic quarters). The core course work is the same for all four sequences: two academic quarters spent mostly in intensive reporting and writing.

Then the curriculum diverges depending on your sequence. In the new media program, students take a course in new media production tools and then spend an entire academic quarter immersed in our new media publishing project class. In this class, they work in teams and are asked to apply new media technologies to create some combination of content and services that fulfill an audience need and take advantage of the unique capabilities of new media.

Q. What are the main differences between electronic and print journalism?

A. Traditionally electronic journalism has referred to television and radio. The main differences between TV/radio and print are twofold. First, because of audience and commercial considerations, in general, TV/radio journalism puts a premium on brevity, so it is a difficult medium for covering a story in depth. Second, because broadcast stories need media assets (video, audio), there is more work involved in information gathering as well as production of the story. This makes the reporter's job more complicated and often requires them to work in a team environment (camera person, producer, etc.). But the storytelling power of audio and video can be enormous, and broadcast journalism reaches larger audiences.

New media journalism is in some ways similar to TV/radio journalism, in that you can use multimedia in telling your story and often are working in a team production environment. But it also shares characteristics of print, because new media stories can have strong text components, and can go into a subject in great depth. But the single characteristic of new media journalism that makes it unique is that it is interactive—meaning the user/viewer is in control of the experience. That is a powerful attribute, in that it offers the possibility of engaging the user/viewer in ways traditional media cannot. But it is also troublesome, for at least two reasons. First, the user/viewer is always just a click away from leaving your story. And second, because the user has control over how he or she navigates through the story, the structure of the story has to change. A story may still have a beginning, middle and end, but the user may not go through the story in that order. And even if you keep that kind of narrative structure, you also have the opportunity to offer additional material (a video, a slideshow, an interview transcript, an original document, etc.) that can divert their attention from the narrative thread. I don't think it's exaggerating to say that we'll need to invent new ways of storytelling to take advantage of new media, and we have barely begun to do so.

Q. **For what type of jobs does your program prepare students?**
A. I would say that our program serves three types of students:
- Those who are planning to serve as writers or editors for journalistic websites.
- Those who want to go into the production of multimedia journalism (telling a journalistic story using multiple tools—text, photos, audio, video, animation, etc.).
- Those planning to head into a more traditional journalism job (reporter, editor, etc.), but who believe that having a deeper understanding of new media and its implications will prove beneficial to them at some point in their careers.

Q. **What are your primary and secondary job duties as a journalism professor?**
A. My primary responsibility is to develop and teach courses in journalism to students (in my case, both undergraduates and master's students at the Medill School of Journalism). Secondarily, I have administrative/management responsibilities as chair of a department and as director of our graduate program in new media journalism. Finally, and less formally, I advise students and help them figure out a career path upon leaving Medill.

Many of my counterparts at other universities would tell you that their primary or secondary responsibility is to conduct original academic research on journalism topics. That is not true in my case because I am not on the research (tenure) track at Medill. This means I can give my primary focus to students.

Q. **What are the most important qualities for journalism professors?**
A. An interest in working with young people, a passion for journalism, and patience.

Q. **What are some of the pros and cons of your job?**
A. Pros: Only a limited number of hours when I absolutely have to be at a certain place at a certain time (i.e., when my classes are scheduled, faculty meetings, etc.); a great deal of independence and room for creativity in how I approach my teaching; and satisfaction at seeing students apply what they've learned.

Cons: It's not a job you can leave behind when you're not in the classroom or your office. Students want and deserve help at odd hours, and it seems there's always another lecture to prepare or another assignment to grade. It can be frustrating when a student just doesn't "get it" no matter how hard you try, or when they don't care as much about the subject matter as you do. Universities also can be fairly bureaucratic and slow-moving if you want to make changes.

Q. What are the most important qualities for journalism majors today?

A. Curiosity, the ability to write well, adaptability to change, and critical thinking skills

Q. What advice do you give students as they graduate and look for jobs in journalism?

A. The media business, and therefore journalism, is entering a period of enormous change driven by audience behavior, technology, and economics. At least some of the companies that have historically been seen as the best and most successful will have to change or won't survive. But it's an incredibly exciting time as well, and the core skills that journalists have are only becoming more necessary and more valuable. Don't set your heart on working in one particular medium or one particular company. Instead, focus on the mission of journalism: to provide people with information they need to function in a democratic society. And look for ways you can help fulfill that mission. Don't be afraid of change; seek out new opportunities.

Magazine Editors

OVERVIEW

Magazine editors plan the contents of a magazine, assign articles and select photographs and artwork to enhance the message of the articles, and edit, organize, and sometimes rewrite the articles. They are responsible for making sure that each issue is attractive, readable, and maintains the stylistic integrity of the publication. There are approximately 130,000 editors (all types) employed in the United States.

HISTORY

For the most part, the magazines that existed before the 19th century were designed for relatively small, highly educated audiences. In the early 19th century, however, inexpensive magazines that catered to a larger audience began to appear. At the same time, magazines began to specialize, targeting specific audiences. That trend continues today, with more than 17,000 magazines currently in production.

Beginning in the 19th century, magazine staffs became more specialized. Whereas in early publishing a single person would perform various functions, in 19th-century and later publishing, employees performed individual tasks. Instead of having a single editor, for example, a magazine would have an editorial staff. One person would be responsible for acquisitions, another would copyedit, another would be responsible for editorial tasks related to production, and so forth.

The publishing industry has also been powerfully affected by technology. Publishing came into existence only after Gutenberg had invented the necessary technology, and it has changed in various

QUICK FACTS

School Subjects
English
Journalism

Personal Interests
Communication/ideas
Helping/teaching

Work Environment
Primarily indoors
Primarily one location

Minimum Education Level
Bachelor's degree

Salary Range
$24,590 to $41,460 to $85,000+

Certification or Licensing
None available

Outlook
About as fast as the average

DOT
132

GOE
01.02.01

NOC
5122

O*NET-SOC
27-3041.00

ways as technology has developed. The most important recent developments have been those that have made it possible to transfer and manipulate information rapidly and efficiently. The development of the computer has revolutionized the running of magazines and other publications. The worldwide scope of magazine reporting is, of course, dependent upon technology that makes it possible to transmit stories and photographs almost instantaneously from one part of the world to another.

Finally, the Internet has provided an entirely new medium for magazines. Readers can read many magazines online. Online publishers avoid paper and printing costs, but still collect revenue from online subscriptions and advertising.

THE JOB

The duties of a magazine editor are numerous, varied, and unpredictable. The editor determines each article's placement in the magazine, working closely with the sales, art, and production departments to ensure that the publication's components complement one another and are appealing and readable.

Most magazines focus on a particular topic, such as fashion, news, or sports. Current topics of interest in the magazine's specialty area dictate a magazine's content. In some cases, magazines themselves set trends, generating interest in topics that become popular. Therefore, the editor should know the latest trends in the field that the magazine represents.

Depending on the magazine's size, editors may specialize in a particular area. For example, a fashion magazine may have a beauty editor, features editor, short story editor, and fashion editor. Each editor is responsible for acquiring, proofing, rewriting, and sometimes writing articles.

After determining the magazine's contents, the editor assigns articles to writers and photographers. The editor may have a clear vision of the topic or merely a rough outline. In any case, the editor supervises the article from writing through production, assisted by copy editors, assistant editors, fact checkers, researchers, and editorial assistants. The editor also sets a department budget and negotiates contracts with freelance writers, photographers, and artists.

The magazine editor reviews each article, checking it for clarity, conciseness, and reader appeal. Frequently, the editor edits the manuscript to highlight particular items. Sometimes the magazine editor writes an editorial to stimulate discussion or mold public opinion. The editor also may write articles on topics of personal interest.

Other editorial positions at magazines include the *editor in chief*, who is responsible for the overall editorial course of the magazine; the *executive editor*, who controls day-to-day scheduling and operations; and the *managing editor*, who coordinates copy flow and supervises production of master pages for each issue.

Some entry-level jobs in magazine editorial departments are stepping stones to more responsible positions. *Editorial assistants* perform various tasks such as answering phones and correspondence, setting up meetings and photography shoots, checking facts, and typing manuscripts. *Editorial production assistants* assist in coordinating the layout of feature articles edited by editors and art designed by *art directors* to prepare the magazine for printing.

Many magazines hire *freelance writers* to write articles on an assignment or contract basis. Most freelance writers write for several different publications; some become *contributing editors* to one or more publications to which they contribute the bulk of their work.

Magazines also employ *researchers*, sometimes called *fact checkers*, to ensure the factual accuracy of an article's content. Researchers may be on staff or hired on a freelance basis.

REQUIREMENTS
High School
While in high school, develop your writing, reading, and analyzing skills through English and composition classes. It will also benefit you to be current with the latest news and events of the world, so consider taking history or politics classes. Reading the daily newspaper and news magazines can also keep you fresh on current events and will help you to become familiar with different styles of journalistic writing.

If your school offers journalism classes or, better yet, has a school newspaper, get involved. Any participation in the publishing process will be great experience, whether you are writing articles, proofreading copy, or laying out pages.

Postsecondary Training
A college degree is required for entry into this field. A degree in journalism, English, or communications is the most popular and standard degree for a magazine editor. Specialized publications prefer a degree in the magazine's specialty, such as chemistry for a chemistry

Editors of *Forbes* discuss the magazine's next issue. *(James Leynse/Corbis)*

magazine, and experience in writing and editing. A broad liberal arts background is important for work at any magazine.

Most colleges and universities offer specific courses in magazine design, writing, editing, and photography. Related courses might include newspaper and book editing.

Other Requirements

All entry-level positions in magazine publishing require a working knowledge of typing and word processing, plus a superior command of grammar, punctuation, and spelling. Deadlines are important, so commitment, organization, and resourcefulness are crucial.

Editing is intellectually stimulating work that may involve investigative techniques in politics, history, and business. Magazine editors must be talented wordsmiths with impeccable judgment. Their decisions about which opinions, editorials, or essays to feature may influence a large number of people.

EXPLORING

The best way to get a sense of magazine editing is to work on a high school newspaper or newsletter. You will probably start out as a staff writer, but with time and experience, you may be able to move into an editorial position with more responsibility and freedom to choose the topics to cover.

EMPLOYERS

Approximately 130,000 editors of all types are employed in the United States. Major magazines are concentrated in New York, Chicago, Los Angeles, Boston, Philadelphia, San Francisco, and Washington, D.C., while professional, technical, and union publications are spread throughout the country.

STARTING OUT

Competition for editorial jobs can be fierce, especially in the popular magazine industry. Recent graduates hoping to break into the business should be willing to work in other staff positions before moving into an editorial position.

Many editors enter the field as editorial assistants or proofreaders. Some editorial assistants perform only clerical tasks, whereas others may also proofread or perform basic editorial tasks. Typically, an editorial assistant who performs well will be given the opportunity to take on more and more editorial duties as time passes. Proofreaders have the advantage of being able to look at the work of editors, so they can learn while they do their own work.

Good sources of information about job openings are school placement offices and classified ads in newspapers, specialized publications such as *Publishers Weekly* (http://www.publishersweekly.com), and corporate and career-oriented websites.

ADVANCEMENT

Employees who start as editorial assistants or proofreaders and show promise generally become copy editors. Copy editors work their way up to become senior editors, managing editors, and editors in chief. In many cases, magazine editors advance by moving from a position on one magazine to the same position with a larger or more prestigious magazine. Such moves often bring significant increases in both pay and status.

EARNINGS

According to the U.S. Department of Labor, the median annual earnings for salaried editors were $41,460 in 2003. The middle 50 percent earned between $31,280 and $56,910. Salaries ranged from less than $24,590 to more than $77,430. Senior editors at large-circulation magazines average more than $85,000 a year. In addition, many editors supplement their salaried income by doing freelance work.

Full-time editors receive vacation time, medical insurance, and sick time, but freelancers must provide their own benefits.

WORK ENVIRONMENT

Most magazine editors work in quiet offices or cubicles. However, even in relatively quiet surroundings, editors can face many distractions. An editor who is trying to copyedit or review the editing of others may, for example, have to deal with phone calls or emails from authors, questions from junior editors, meetings with members of the editorial and production staff, and questions from freelancers, among many other demands.

An often stressful part of the magazine editor's job is meeting deadlines. Magazine editors work in a much more pressurized atmosphere than book editors because they face daily or weekly deadlines, whereas book production usually takes place over several months. Many magazine editors must work long hours during certain phases of the publishing cycle.

OUTLOOK

Magazine publishing is a dynamic industry. Magazines are launched every day of the year, although the majority fail. According to Magazine Publishers of America, 289 new magazines were introduced in 2002. The organization names the Internet, government affairs, and consumer marketing as some of the important issues currently facing the magazine publishing industry. The future of magazines is secure since they are a critical medium for advertisers.

A recent trend in magazine publishing is focus on a special interest. There is increasing opportunity for employment at special interest, trade, and association magazines for those whose backgrounds complement a magazine's specialty. Internet publishing will provide increasing job opportunities as more businesses develop online publications. Magazine editing is keenly competitive, however, and as with any career, the applicant with the most education and experience has a better chance of getting the job. The *Occupational Outlook Handbook* projects average employment growth for editors and writers through 2012.

FOR MORE INFORMATION

For membership information, contact
American Society of Magazine Editors
810 Seventh Avenue, 24th Floor
New York, NY 10019
Tel: 212-872-3700
http://asme.magazine.org

For industry statistics, information on diversity, and to view a PowerPoint presentation entitled "Tips on Finding a Job in Magazines" visit the MPA website.
Magazine Publishers of America (MPA)
810 Seventh Avenue, 24th Floor
New York, NY 10019
Tel: 212-872-3700
Email: mpa@magazine.org
http://www.magazine.org

For comprehensive information for citizens, students, and news people about the field of journalism, visit
Project for Excellence in Journalism and the Committee of Concerned Journalists
http://www.journalism.org

News Anchors

QUICK FACTS

School Subjects
English
Journalism
Speech

Personal Skills
Communication/ideas
Leadership/management

Work Environment
Primarily indoors
Primarily one location

Minimum Education Level
Bachelor's degree

Salary Range
$10,000 to $20,940 to
$1 million+

Certification or Licensing
None available

Outlook
Decline

DOT
131

GOE
11.08.03

NOC
5231

O*NET-SOC
27-3011.00

OVERVIEW

News anchors analyze and broadcast news for radio and television stations. They help select, write, and present the news and may specialize in a particular area. Interviewing guests, making public service announcements, and conducting panel discussions may also be part of the news anchor's work. Approximately 76,000 people are employed as announcers (including news anchors) at radio and television stations in the United States.

HISTORY

Guglielmo Marconi, a young Italian engineer, first transmitted a radio signal in his home in 1895. Radio developed rapidly as people began to comprehend the tremendous possibilities. The stations KDKA in Pittsburgh and WWWJ in Detroit began broadcasting in 1920. Within 10 years, there were radio stations in all the major cities in the United States, and broadcasting became big business. In 1926 the National Broadcasting Company became the first network when it linked together 25 stations across the country. The Columbia Broadcasting System was organized in the following year. In 1934, the Mutual Broadcasting Company was founded. The years between 1930 and 1950 may be considered the zenith years of the radio industry. With the coming of television, radio broadcasting took second place in importance as entertainment for the home—but radio's commercial and communications value should not be underestimated.

Discoveries that led to the development of television can be traced as far back as 1878, when William Crookes invented a tube that produced the cathode ray. Other inventors who contributed to the development of television were Vladimir Zworykin, a Russian-born scientist who came to this country at the age of 20 and is credited with inventing the iconoscope before he was 30; Charles Jenkins, who invented a scanning disk, using certain vacuum tubes and photoelectric cells; and Philo Farnsworth, who invented an image dissector. WNBT and WCBW, the first commercially licensed television stations, went on the air in 1941 in New York. Both suspended operations during World War II but resumed them in 1946 when television sets began to be manufactured on a commercial scale.

As radio broadcasting was growing across the country in its early days, the need for news anchors grew. They identified the station and brought continuity to broadcast time by linking one program with the next as well as participating in many programs. When television began, many radio announcers and newscasters started to work in the new medium. The emergence of cable television and the Internet has opened up new opportunities for news anchors.

THE JOB

News anchors specialize in presenting the news to the listening or viewing public. They report the facts and may sometimes be asked to provide editorial commentary. They may write their own scripts or rely on the station's writing team to write the script, which they then read over the TelePrompTer. Research is important to each news story and the news anchors should be well-informed about each story they cover as well as those they simply introduce. News anchors may also report the news, produce special segments, and conduct on-the-air interviews and panel discussions. At small stations, they may even keep the program log, run the transmitter, and cue the changeover to network broadcasting.

News anchors are faced with constant deadlines, not only for each newscast to begin, but also for each one to end. Each segment must be viewed and each script must be read at the precise time and for a specified duration during the newscast. While they must appear calm, professional, and confident, there is often much stress and tension behind the scenes.

Although they perform similar jobs, radio and television news anchors work in very different atmospheres. On radio, the main announcers or anchorpeople are also the *disc jockeys*. They play recorded music, announce the news, provide informal commentary, and serve as a bridge between the music and the listener. They

Top Television Markets

1. New York, N.Y.
2. Los Angeles, Calif.
3. Chicago, Ill.
4. Philadelphia, Pa.
5. San Francisco-Oakland-San Jose, Calif.

Source: Nielsen Media Research

Top Radio Markets

1. New York, N.Y.
2. Los Angeles, Calif.
3. Chicago, Ill.
4. San Francisco, Calif.
5. Dallas-Ft. Worth, Tex.

Source: Arbitron

announce the time, weather, news, and traffic reports while maintaining a cheerful and relaxed attitude. At most stations, the radio announcers also read advertising information or provide the voices for the advertising spots.

For *television news anchors,* research, writing, and presenting the news is only part of the job. Wardrobe, make-up, and presentation are major components of a television anchor's job. Many details such as which hairstyles and which outfits to wear are important to create an effective look for the news.

Some radio or television news anchors specialize in certain aspects of the news such as health, economics, politics, or community affairs. Other anchors specialize in sports. These people cover sports events and must be highly knowledgeable about the sports they are covering as well as having an ability to describe events quickly and accurately as they unfold. *Sports anchors* generally travel to the events they cover and spend time watching the teams or individuals practice and participate. They research background information, statistics, ratings, and personal interest information to provide the audience with the most thorough and interesting coverage of each sports event.

The Internet and the World Wide Web are changing the job of news anchors in radio and television. Many radio and television stations have their own websites where listeners and viewers can keep updated on current stories, email comments and suggestions, and even interact with the anchors and reporters. Also, the World Wide Web has become another resource for anchors as they research their stories.

Because their voices and faces are heard and seen by the public on a daily basis, many radio and television news anchors become well-known public personalities. This means that they are often asked to participate in community activities and other public events.

REQUIREMENTS

High School

In high school, you should focus on a college preparatory curriculum that will teach you how to write and speak and use the English language in literature and communication classes. Subjects such as history, government, economics, and a foreign language are also important. Participation in journalism clubs and on your school newspaper will also help you prepare for this career.

Postsecondary Training

Today, most news anchors have earned at least a bachelor's degree in journalism, English, political science, economics, telecommunications, or communications. Visit the website of the Accrediting Council on Education in Journalism and Mass Communications (http://www. ku.edu/~acejmc/STUDENT/PROGLIST.SHTML) for a list of accredited postsecondary training programs in journalism and mass communications.

Other Requirements

Aspiring radio and television news anchors must have a mastery of the English language—both written and spoken. Their diction, including correct grammar usage, pronunciation, and minimal regional dialect, is extremely important. News anchors need to have a pleasing personality and voice, and, in the case of television anchorpeople, they must also have a pleasing appearance.

News anchors need to be creative, inquisitive, aggressive, and should know how to meet and interact with people—including coworkers and people who they interview to help gather the news.

EXPLORING

If you are interested in a career as a news anchor, try to get a summer job at a radio or television station. Although you will probably not have the opportunity to broadcast, you may be able to judge whether or not the type of work appeals to you as a career.

Any chance to speak or perform before an audience should be welcomed. Join the speech or debate team to build strong speaking skills. Appearing as a speaker or performer can show whether or not you have the stage presence necessary for a career in front of a microphone or camera.

Many colleges and universities have their own radio and television stations and offer courses in radio and television. You can gain valuable experience working at college-owned stations. Some radio stations, cable systems, and TV stations offer financial assistance, internships, and co-op work programs, as well as scholarships and fellowships.

EMPLOYERS

Of the roughly 76,000 announcers (including news anchors) working in the United States, almost all are on staff at one of the 13,563 radio stations or 1,733 television stations around the country. Some, however, work on a freelance basis on individual assignments for networks, stations, advertising agencies, and other producers of commercials.

Some companies own several television or radio stations; some stations belong to networks such as ABC, CBS, NBC, or FOX, while others are independent. While radio and television stations are located throughout the United States, major markets where better-paying jobs are found are generally near large metropolitan areas.

STARTING OUT

Most news anchors start in jobs such as production assistant, researcher, or reporter in small stations. As opportunities arise, it is common for anchors to move from one job to another. Network jobs are few, and the competition for them is great. You must have several years of experience as well as a college education to be considered for these positions.

You must audition before you will be employed as a news anchor. You should carefully select audition material to show a prospective employer the full range of your abilities. In addition to presenting prepared materials, you may be asked to read material that you have not seen previously, such as a commercial, news release, dramatic selection, or poem.

ADVANCEMENT

Radio and television news anchors move up by moving on. In other words, one of the main ways to advance within the industry is to move to a larger market or larger station. The ultimate goal of many news anchors is to advance to the network level. Others advance by becoming news directors, station managers, or producers.

EARNINGS

According to the *2002 Radio and Television Salary Survey* by the Radio-Television News Directors Association, there is a wide range of salaries for news anchors. For radio news anchors, the median salary was $27,500 with a low of $10,000 and a high of $150,000. For television news anchors, the median salary was $50,000 with a low of $17,000 and a high of $1 million.

Median annual earnings of all announcers (including news anchors) were $20,940 in 2003, according to the U.S. Department of Labor. Salaries ranged from less than $12,750 to $52,560 or more.

For both radio and television, salaries are higher in larger markets. Salaries are also generally higher in commercial broadcasting than in public broadcasting. Nationally known news anchors who appear regularly on network television programs receive salaries that may be quite impressive. For those who become top television personalities in large metropolitan areas, salaries also are quite high.

WORK ENVIRONMENT

Work in radio and television stations is usually very pleasant. Almost all stations are housed in modern facilities. The maintenance of technical electronic equipment requires temperature and dust control, and people who work around such equipment benefit from the precautions taken to preserve it.

News anchors' jobs may provide opportunities to meet well-known people or celebrities. Being at the center of an important communications medium can make the broadcaster more keenly aware of current issues and divergent points of view than the average person.

News anchors may report for work at a very early hour in the morning or work late into the night. Some radio stations operate on a 24-hour basis. All-night news anchors may be alone in the station during their working hours.

OUTLOOK

Competition for entry-level employment in announcing during the coming years is expected to be keen, as the broadcasting industry always attracts more applicants than are needed to fill available openings. There is a better chance of working in radio than in television because there are more radio stations. Local television stations usually carry a high percentage of network programs and need only a very small staff to carry out local operations.

The U.S. Department of Labor predicts that opportunities for announcers (including news anchors) will decline through 2012 due to the slowing growth of new radio and television stations. Openings will result mainly from those who leave the industry or the labor force. The trend among major networks, and to some extent among many smaller radio and TV stations, is toward specialization. News anchors who specialize in such areas as business, sports, weather, consumer, and health news should have an advantage over other job applicants.

FOR MORE INFORMATION

For a list of accredited programs in journalism and mass communications, visit the ACEJMC website.

Accrediting Council on Education in Journalism and Mass
    Communications (ACEJMC)
University of Kansas School of Journalism
    and Mass Communications
Stauffer-Flint Hall, 1435 Jayhawk Boulevard
Lawrence, KS 66045-7575
http://www.ku.edu/~acejmc/STUDENT/PROGLIST.SHTML

For a list of schools offering degrees in broadcasting as well as scholarship information, contact

Broadcast Education Association
1771 N Street, NW
Washington, DC 20036-2891
Tel: 888-380-7222
Email: beainfo@beaweb.org
http://www.beaweb.org

For college programs and union information, contact

National Association of Broadcast Employees and Technicians
501 Third Street, NW, 8th Floor
Washington, DC 20001
Tel: 202-434-1254
Email: nabet@nabetcwa.org
http://nabetcwa.org

For broadcast education and scholarship information, contact
National Association of Broadcasters
1771 N Street, NW
Washington, DC 20036
Tel: 202-429-5300
Email: nab@nab.org
http://www.nab.org

For information on farm broadcasting, contact
National Association of Farm Broadcasters
PO Box 500
Platte City, MO 64079
Tel: 816-431-4032
http://www.nafb.com

For scholarship and internship information, contact
Radio-Television News Directors Association
Radio-Television News Directors Foundation
1600 K Street, NW, Suite 700
Washington, DC 20006-2838
Tel: 202-659-6510
Email: rtnda@rtnda.org
http://www.rtnda.org

For comprehensive information for citizens, students, and news people about the field of journalism, visit
Project for Excellence in Journalism and the Committee of Concerned Journalists
http://www.journalism.org

Newspaper Editors

QUICK FACTS

School Subjects
English
Journalism

Personal Interests
Communication/ideas
Helping/teaching

Work Environment
Primarily indoors
Primarily one location

Minimum Education Level
Bachelor's degree

Salary Range
$24,590 to $47,260 to
$77,430+

Certification or Licensing
None available

Outlook
About as fast as the average

DOT
132

GOE
01.02.01

NOC
5122

O*NET-SOC
27-3041.00

OVERVIEW

Newspaper editors assign, review, edit, rewrite, and lay out all copy in a newspaper except advertisements. Editors sometimes write stories or editorials that offer opinions on issues. Editors review the editorial page and copy written by staff or syndicated columnists. A large metropolitan daily newspaper staff may include various editors who process thousands of words into print daily. A small town staff of a weekly newspaper, however, may include only one editor, who might be both owner and star reporter. Large metropolitan areas such as New York, Los Angeles, Chicago, and Washington, D.C., employ many editors. Approximately 130,000 editors work for publications of all types in the United States.

HISTORY

Journalism may have begun in Rome with the regular publication of reports called *Acta Diurna,* or *Daily Acts,* begun in 59 B.C. They reported political news and social events on a daily basis. In China, a journal called the *pao* was published on a regular basis from A.D. 618 until 1911, recording activities of the court. The first regularly printed European newspapers appeared in the early 1700s in Germany, The Netherlands, and Italy. The Dutch *corantos,* composed of items from the foreign press, were translated into English and French around 1620. The first English newspaper is considered to be the *Weekly Newes,* initially published in 1622. Until 1644, the news in English journals was controlled by the Star Chamber, a court that censored any unfavorable information about the king. Interestingly, also in 1644, the chamber was dismissed, and the English enjoyed the first semblance of freedom of the press. It was not until 1670 that the term "newspaper" came into use.

Benjamin Harris, an English journalist who immigrated to the United States, published the first American colonial newspaper in Boston in 1690, but because of the repressive climate of the times, it was immediately closed down by the British governor.

The first regularly circulated newspaper in the colonies was the *Boston News-Letter,* a weekly first published in 1704 by John Campbell. The press at this time still operated under rather severe government restrictions, but the struggle for freedom of the press grew, and before the end of the century, journalists were able to print the news without fear of repression.

The need for newspaper editors grew rapidly through the 19th and early 20th centuries as the demand for newspapers grew, causing circulation to jump from thousands to millions. New technology allowed the newspaper industry to meet the demand. Presses were invented that could produce newspapers by the millions on a daily basis.

In the 19th century, newspaper publishers began to endorse political candidates and to take stands on other political and social issues. They also came to be sources of entertainment. When Benjamin Day founded the *New York Sun* in 1833, he sought to do more than inform. The paper's pages were filled with news from the police beat as well as gossip, disasters, animal stories, and anecdotes. Other papers of the era began to print sports news, particularly horse racing and prize fights, society pages, and the business news from Wall Street. By the mid-19th century, there was an outpouring of human interest news, and journalists discovered the public appetite for scandal. By the end of the century, a number of newspaper editors were famed for their craft, including Horace Greeley of the *New York Tribune,* Charles A. Dana of the *New York Sun,* and William Allen White of the *Kansas Gazette.*

Newspaper sensationalism reached its peak during the last years of the 19th century and the first decades of the 20th. The most notable figure in this period of "yellow journalism" was William Randolph Hearst. He built a vast newspaper empire by playing on the emotions of his readership. Hearst often fabricated news, as did others, including his chief rival of the period, Joseph Pulitzer of the *New York World.* Perhaps the most glaring example of this type of journalism was Hearst and Pulitzer's exaggerated treatment of Spanish atrocities in Cuba, which incited public sentiment for war against Spain. Historians feel that the news coverage was at least partially responsible for the declaration of war that came in 1898.

Although most newspapers through the 20th century have adhered to ethical journalistic practices, a number of dailies and weekly tabloids, protected by freedom of the press, continue to exploit the sensationalist market. Journalists in general, however, have adopted codes, such as that of the Society of Professional Journalists, which stress responsibility, freedom of the press, ethics, accuracy, objectivity, and fair play.

By the 20th century, newspapers became big business. Many newspaper publishing companies became corporate conglomerates that owned printing plants, radio and television stations, paper plants, forest acreage, and other related assets. Most of the profits came from advertising dollars as newspapers became the leading medium for advertising. As costs rose, it took more and more advertising to support the news portion of the paper, until advertising occupied most of the space in almost all U.S. newspapers. The amount of advertising, in most cases, now determines the amount of news coverage a newspaper carries. Eventually, many newspapers could not withstand the rising costs and the increased competition from television. From the mid-20th century newspapers started declining at a rapid rate. Between 1962 and 1990, for instance, the number of daily papers in the United States fell from 1,761 to 1,626.

As some papers failed, others, especially in large cities, grew as they took over new circulation. The major metropolitan dailies continued to add new and more exciting features in order to keep up with the competition, especially television.

From the beginning of the century, newspapers had been expanding their coverage, and on large papers, editorial departments came to be divided into many specialty areas, requiring reporters and editors with equivalent specialties. Today, most newspapers have departments devoted to entertainment, sports, business, science, consumer affairs, education, and just about every other area of interest in today's society. Many also have an online version that features articles from print editions as well as Internet exclusives.

THE JOB

Newspaper editors are responsible for the paper's entire news content. The news section includes features, "hard" news, and editorial commentary. Editors of a daily paper plan the contents of each day's issue, assigning articles, reviewing submissions, prioritizing stories, checking wire services, selecting illustrations, and laying out each page with the advertising space allotted.

At a large daily newspaper, an *editor in chief* oversees the entire editorial operation, determines its editorial policy, and reports to the publisher. The *managing editor* is responsible for day-to-day operations in an administrative capacity. *Story editors,* or *wire editors,* determine which national news agency (or wire service) stories will be used and edit them. Wire services give smaller papers, without foreign correspondents, access to international stories.

A *city editor* gathers local and sometimes state and national news. The city editor hires copy editors and reporters, hands out assignments to reporters and photographers, reviews and edits stories, confers with executive editors on story content and space availability, and gives stories to copy editors for final editing.

A newspaper may have separate desks for state, national, and foreign news, each with its own head editor. Some papers have separate *editorial page editors.* The *department editors* oversee individual features; they include *business editors, fashion editors, sports editors, book section editors, entertainment editors,* and more. Department heads make decisions on coverage, recommend story ideas, and make assignments. They often have backgrounds in their department's subject matter and are highly skilled at writing and editing.

The copy desk, the story's last stop, is staffed by *copy editors,* who correct spelling, grammar, and punctuation mistakes; check for readability and sense; edit for clarification; examine stories for factual accuracy; and ensure the story conforms to editorial policy. Copy editors sometimes write headlines or picture captions and may crop photos. Occasionally they find serious problems that cause them to send stories back to the editors or the writer.

Editors, particularly copy editors, base many of their decisions on a style book that provides preferences in spelling, grammar, and word usage; it indicates when to use foreign spellings or English translations and the preferred system of transliteration. Some houses develop their own style books, but often they use or adapt the *Associated Press Stylebook.*

After editors approve the story's organization, coverage, writing quality, and accuracy, they turn it over to the *news editors,* who supervise article placement and determine page layout with the advertising department. News and executive editors discuss the relative priorities of major news stories. If a paper is divided into several sections, each has its own priorities.

Modern newspaper editors depend heavily on computers. Generally, a reporter types the story directly onto the computer network, providing editors with immediate access. Some editorial departments are situated remotely from printing facilities, but computers allow the printer to receive copy immediately upon approval. Today, designers computerize page layout. Many columnists send their finished columns from home computers to the editorial department via modem.

REQUIREMENTS

High School

English is the most important school subject for any future editor. You must have a strong grasp of the English language, including vocabulary, grammar, and punctuation, and you must be able to write well in various styles. Study journalism and take communications-related courses. Work as a writer or editor for your school paper or yearbook. Computer classes that teach word processing software and how to navigate the Internet will be invaluable in your future research. You absolutely must learn to type. If you cannot type accurately and rapidly, you will be at an extreme disadvantage.

Editors have knowledge in a wide range of topics, and the more you know about history, geography, math, the sciences, the arts, and culture, the better a writer and editor you will be.

Postsecondary Training

Look for a school with strong journalism and communications programs. Many programs require you to complete two years of liberal arts studies before concentrating on journalism studies. Journalism courses include reporting, writing, and editing; press law and ethics; journalism history; and photojournalism. Advanced classes include feature writing, investigative reporting, and graphics. Some schools offer internships for credit.

When hiring, newspapers look closely at a candidate's extracurricular activities, putting special emphasis on internships, school newspaper and freelance writing and editing, and part-time newspaper work (stringing). Typing, computer skills, and knowledge of printing are helpful.

Other Requirements

To be a successful newspaper editor, you must have a love of learning, reading, and writing. You should enjoy the process of discovering information and presenting it to a wide audience in a complete, precise, and understandable way. You must be detail-oriented and care about the finer points of accuracy, not only in writing, but in reporting and presentation. You must be able to work well with coworkers, both giving and taking direction, and you must be able to work alone. Editors can spend long hours sitting at a desk in front of a computer screen.

EXPLORING

One of the best ways to explore this job is by working on your school's newspaper or other publication. You will most probably start as a staff writer or proofreader, but the experience will help you understand editing and how it relates to the entire field of publishing.

Keeping a journal is another good way to polish your writing skills and explore your interest in writing and editing your own work. In fact, any writing project will be helpful, since editing and writing are inextricably linked. Make an effort to write every day, even if it is only a few paragraphs. Try different kinds of writing, such as letters to the editor, short stories, poetry, essays, comedic prose, and plays.

EMPLOYERS

There are approximately 130,000 editors in the United States. Generally, newspaper editors are employed in every city or town, as most towns have at least one newspaper. As the population multiplies, so do the opportunities. In large metropolitan areas, there may be one or two daily papers, several general-interest weekly papers, ethnic and other special-interest newspapers, trade newspapers, and daily and weekly community and suburban newspapers. All of these publications need managing and department editors. Online papers also provide opportunities for editors.

STARTING OUT

A typical route of entry into this field is by working as an editorial assistant or proofreader. Editorial assistants perform clerical tasks as well as some proofreading and other basic editorial tasks. Proofreaders can learn about editorial jobs while they work on a piece by looking at editors' comments on their work.

Job openings can be found using school placement offices, classified ads in newspapers and trade journals, and specialized publications such as *Publishers Weekly* (http://www.publishersweekly.com). The American Society of Newspaper Editors also has links to job listings at its website, http://www.asne.org. In addition, many publishers have websites that list job openings, and large publishers often have telephone job lines that serve the same purpose.

ADVANCEMENT

Newspaper editors generally begin working on the copy desk, where they progress from less significant stories and projects to major news and feature stories. A common route to advancement is for copy editors to be promoted to a particular department, where they may move up the ranks to management positions. An editor who has achieved success in a department may become a city editor, who is responsible for news, or a managing editor, who runs the entire editorial operation of a newspaper.

EARNINGS

Salaries for newspaper editors vary from small to large communities, but editors generally are well compensated. Other factors affecting compensation include quality of education and previous experience, job level, and the newspaper's circulation. Large metropolitan dailies offer higher-paying jobs, while outlying weekly papers pay less.

According to the U.S. Department of Labor, the mean annual income for newspaper, periodical, book, and directory editors was $47,260 in 2003. Salaries for all editors ranged from less than $24,590 to more than $77,430 annually.

On many newspapers, salary ranges and benefits, such as vacation time and health insurance, for most nonmanagerial editorial workers are negotiated by the Newspaper Guild.

WORK ENVIRONMENT

The environments in which editors work vary widely. For the most part, publishers of all kinds realize that a quiet atmosphere is conducive to work that requires tremendous concentration. It takes an unusual ability to edit in a noisy place. Most editors work in private offices or cubicles. Even in relatively quiet surroundings, however, editors often have many distractions. In many cases, editors have computers that are exclusively for their own use, but in others, editors must share computers that are located in a common area.

Deadlines are an important issue for virtually all editors. Newspaper editors work in a much more pressured atmosphere than other editors because they face daily or weekly deadlines. To meet these deadlines, newspaper editors often work long hours. Some newspaper editors start work at 5:00 A.M., others work until

11:00 P.M. or even through the night. Those who work on weekly newspapers, including feature editors, columnists, and editorial page editors, usually work more regular hours.

OUTLOOK

According to the U.S. Department of Labor, employment for editors and writers, while highly competitive, should grow about as fast as the average through 2012. Opportunities will be better on small daily and weekly newspapers, where the pay is lower. Some publications hire freelance editors to support reduced full-time staffs. And as experienced editors leave the workforce or move to other fields, job openings will occur.

FOR MORE INFORMATION

For a list of accredited programs in journalism and mass communications, visit the ACEJMC website.

**Accrediting Council on Education in Journalism and Mass
    Communications (ACEJMC)**
University of Kansas School of Journalism
    and Mass Communications
Stauffer-Flint Hall, 1435 Jayhawk Boulevard
Lawrence, KS 66045-7575
http://www.ku.edu/~acejmc/STUDENT/PROGLIST.SHTML

The ASNE helps editors maintain the highest standards of quality, improve their craft, and better serve their communities. It preserves and promotes core journalistic values. Visit its website to read online publications such as Why Choose Journalism? *and* Preparing for a Career in Newspapers.

American Society of Newspaper Editors (ASNE)
11690B Sunrise Valley Drive
Reston, VA 20191-1409
Tel: 703-453-1122
Email: asne@asne.org
http://www.asne.org

Founded in 1958 by the Wall Street Journal *to improve the quality of journalism education, this organization offers internships, scholarships, and literature for college students. To read* The Journalist's Road to Success: A Career Guide, *which lists schools offering degrees in news-editing, and financial aid to those interested in print journalism, visit the DJNF website:*

Dow Jones Newspaper Fund (DJNF)
PO Box 300
Princeton, NJ 08543-0300
Tel: 609-452-2820
Email: newsfund@wsj.dowjones.com
http://djnewspaperfund.dowjones.com/fund

This trade association for African American–owned newspapers has a foundation that offers a scholarship and internship program for inner-city high school juniors.

National Newspaper Publishers Association
3200 13th Street, NW
Washington, DC 20010
Tel: 202-588-8764
http://www.nnpa.org

This organization for journalists has campus and online chapters.

Society of Professional Journalists
Eugene S. Pulliam National Journalism Center
3909 North Meridian Street
Indianapolis, IN 46208
Tel: 317-927-8000
Email: questions@spj.org
http://spj.org

Visit the following website for comprehensive information on journalism careers, summer programs, and college journalism programs.

High School Journalism
http://www.highschooljournalism.org

For comprehensive information for citizens, students, and news people about the field of journalism, visit

Project for Excellence in Journalism and the Committee of Concerned Journalists
http://www.journalism.org

―――――――――――― **INTERVIEW** ――――――――――――

Don Wycliff has been the public editor of the Chicago Tribune *since 2000. He has held many top positions during his more than 30 years in the newspaper industry, including editorial page editor of the* Tribune *and editorial board member of the* New York Times. *In 1996, Wycliff was a finalist for the Pulitzer Prize in editorial writing. The next year, he won the American Society of Newspaper Editors Distinguished Writing Award for editorials. He was kind enough to discuss his career and the field of newspaper journalism with the editors of* Careers in Focus: Journalism.

Q. Why made you decide to become a newspaper journalist?

A. I decided to become a journalist because I was impressed with the way the Chicago media ferreted out and reported the truth of the December 4, 1969, "shootout" between the Chicago police and the members of the Black Panther Party. I wanted at first to go into TV journalism. But I was unable to find a job in TV and so I took a newspaper job. It wasn't long before I realized I liked newspapering more, because of the depth to which one could go in stories and the fact that one could work alone.

Q. How/where did you get your first job in the field?

A. Houston, Texas, at the *Houston Post,* which now is defunct. I was an intern or "trainee," as they called me. An on-the-job training project.

Q. How have newspaper audiences changed since you began your career?

A. They're smarter, better educated, more partisan and bitter. They have many more choices of sources for news, which is both good and bad.

Q. What are your primary and secondary job duties as public editor?

A. Primary:
- write column explaining editorial decisions
- supervise errors/corrections/accuracy policy
- serve as staff ethics coach

Secondary:
- speak to school, college, and community groups
- talk to the press

Q. What is the most important professional quality for public editors?

A. A diplomatic attitude.

Q. What are some of the pros and cons of your job?

A. The worst of the cons is that I have to hold my tongue, even with people who are uncivil. The best of the pros is that I get to write a column and express my personal point of view.

Q. During your tenure as editorial page editor, the *Tribune* editorial page won a Pulitzer Prize as well as other major awards. What are the key components of an award-winning editorial page?

A. A talented, committed staff; an editorial page editor who respects his staff's intelligence and commitment; and an editor and a publisher willing to give the editorial page staff the freedom to do its job well.

Q. What advice would you give high school students who are interested in entering newspaper journalism?

A. Read widely and voraciously. Write for publication at every opportunity. Be passionate about public affairs and the duties of citizenship in a democracy. Be not afraid.

Photo Editors

OVERVIEW

Photo editors are responsible for the look of final photographs to be published in a book or periodical or that are posted on the Internet. They make photo assignments, judge and alter pictures to meet assignment needs, and make sure all deadlines are met. They work for publishers, advertising agencies, photo stock agencies, greeting card companies, and any employer that relies heavily on visual images to sell its products or services.

HISTORY

For as long as photos have been in print, photo editors have been needed to evaluate them and delegate shooting assignments. In the early days of photography (the late 1800s), the jobs of photographer and editor were generally combined. On the staffs of early newspapers, it was not uncommon to have a story editor evaluate and place photos, or for a reporter to shoot his or her own accompanying photos as well as edit them for print. However, the need for a separate photo editor has become apparent as visual elements have become a larger part of print and online publications, advertisements, and even political campaigns. The trained eye and technical know-how of a photo editor is now an essential part of newsroom staffs and corporate offices everywhere.

QUICK FACTS

School Subjects
Art
Computer science
Journalism

Personal Skills
Artistic
Communication/ideas

Work Environment
Primarily indoors
Primarily one location

Minimum Education Level
Some postsecondary training

Salary Range
$25,000 to $52,864 to $60,889+

Certification or licensing
None available

Outlook
About as fast as the average

DOT
143

GOE
N/A

NOC
5221

O*NET-SOC
N/A

THE JOB

The final look of a print or online publication is the result of many workers. The photo editor is responsible for the pictures you see in these publications. They work with photographers, reporters, authors, copy editors, and company executives to make sure final photos help to illustrate, enlighten, or inspire the reader.

Photo editors, though knowledgeable in photography, generally leave the shooting to staff or contract photographers. Editors meet with their managers or clients to determine the needs of the project and brainstorm ideas for photos that will meet the project's goals. After picture ideas have been discussed, editors give photographers assignments, always including a firm deadline for completion. Most editors work for companies that face firm deadlines; if the editor doesn't have pictures to work with in time, the whole project is held up.

Once photos have arrived, the editor gets to work, using computer software to crop or enlarge shots, alter the coloring of images, or emphasize the photographer's use of shadows or light. All this work requires knowledge of photography, an aesthetic eye, and an awareness of the project's needs. Editors working for a newspaper must be sure to print photos that are true to life, while editors working for a fine-arts publication can alter images to create a more abstract effect.

Photo editors also use photo stock agencies to meet project needs. Depending on the size and type of company the editor works for, he or she might not have a staff of photographers to work with. Stock agencies fill this need. Editors can browse stock photos for sale online or in brochures. Even with purchased photos, the editor still has to make sure the image fits the needs and space of the project.

In addition to working with photos, editors take on managerial tasks, such as assigning deadlines, organizing the office, ordering supplies, training employees, and overseeing the work of others. Along with copy and project editors, the photo editor is in contact with members of upper management or outside clients, and thus he or she is responsible for communicating their needs and desires with other workers.

REQUIREMENTS
High School
In addition to photography classes, take illustration and other art classes to develop an artistic eye and familiarize yourself with other forms of visual aids that are used in publications. Math classes will come in handy, as editors have to exactly measure the size and resolution of photos. To be able to determine what photo will meet the

needs of a project, you will have to do a lot of reading, so English and communications classes are useful. Last but certainly not least, computer science classes will be invaluable. As an editor, you will work with computers almost daily and must be comfortable with art, layout, and word processing programs.

Postsecondary Training

While not required, most large and prestigious companies will want editors with a college degree in photography, visual art, or computer science. Employers will also want experience, so be sure to get as much exposure working on a publication as possible while in school. Other options are to go to a community college for a degree program; many offer programs in art or computer science that should be sufficient.

You should also be more than familiar with photo editing software such as Adobe Photoshop, Apple iPhoto, Corel Photo-Paint, Procreate Painter, and Jasc Paint Shop, just to name a few.

Other Requirements

In addition to technical know-how, you should also be adept at working with people and for people. As an editor, you will often be the liaison between the client or upper management and the reporters and photographers working for you. You need to be able to communicate the needs of the project to all those working on it.

EXPLORING

To see if this career might be for you, explore your interests. Get involved with your school yearbook or newspaper. Both of these publications often appoint student photo editors to assist with photo acquisitions and layout. You should also try your hand at photography. To be a knowledgeable and successful editor, you need to know the medium in which you work.

You could also try to speak to a professional photo editor about his or her work. Ask a teacher or your counselor to set up a meeting, and think of questions to ask the editor ahead of time.

EMPLOYERS

Photo editors work for any organization that produces publications or online newsletters or has a website with many photos. This includes publishing houses, large corporations, website developers, nonprofit organizations, and the government. A large percentage of photo editors also work for stock photo agencies, either as staff photographers or as freelancers.

STARTING OUT

Photo editors often start out as photographers, staff writers, or other lower-level editors. They have to gain experience in their area of work, whether it is magazine publishing or website development, to be able to choose the right photos for their projects.

ADVANCEMENT

Photo editors advance by taking on more supervisory responsibility for their department or by working on larger projects for high-end clients. These positions generally command more money and can lead to chief editorial jobs. Freelance editors advance by working for more clients and charging more money for their services.

EARNINGS

Earnings for photo editors will vary depending on where they work. Salary.com reports that in June 2004, the median expected salary for a typical photo editor was approximately $52,864, but it ranged from less than $45,722 to more than $60,889. Entry-level positions are the same as those for other editorial positions, which is in the range of $25,000 to $30,000. If the editor is employed by a corporation, stock photo agency, or other business, he or she typically will be entitled to health insurance, vacation time, and other benefits. Self-employed editors have to provide their own health and life insurance, but they can make their own schedules.

WORK ENVIRONMENT

Editors typically work in a comfortable office setting, with computers and other tools nearby. Depending on the workplace, the environment can be quiet and slow or busy with plenty of interruptions. Deadline pressures can make the job of photo editing hectic at times. Tight production schedules may leave editors with little time to acquire photos or contract work out to photographers. Editors may have a quick turnaround time from when completed photos land on their desk to when the publication has to be sent to the printer. However, unless the editor works for a daily paper or weekly magazine, these busy periods are generally accompanied by slower periods with looser schedules. A good photo editor is flexible and able to work under both conditions.

OUTLOOK

Photo editing has been a popular and in-demand field for many years. More and more companies are relying on Web presence, complete with engaging visuals, to sell their products or services. Photo editors will also always be needed to help create a polished look to a printed publication, selecting just the right photos to deliver the right message to readers.

Though computers have revolutionized the way that photo editors work—bringing their work from paper to screen—they have also caused some problems. Improved software technology now makes it possible for virtually anyone to scan or download an image and alter it to any specifications. However, most professional publications will still hire photo editors with expertise and a trained eye to do this work.

FOR MORE INFORMATION

The NPPA maintains a job bank, provides educational information, and makes insurance available to its members. It also publishes News Photographer *magazine.*

National Press Photographers Association (NPPA)
3200 Croasdaile Drive, Suite 306
Durham, NC 27705
Tel: 919-383-7246
Email: info@nppa.org
http://www.nppa.org

This organization provides training, publishes its own magazine, and offers various services for its members.

Professional Photographers of America
229 Peachtree Street, NE, Suite 2200
Atlanta, GA 30303
Tel: 800-786-6277
Email: csc@ppa.com
http://www.ppa.com

This organization provides workshops, conferences, and other professional meetings for "management or leadership-level people responsible for overseeing photography at their publications." Visit its website to read articles on news and developments within the industry.

Associated Press Photo Managers
Email: appm@ap.org
http://www.apphotomanagers.org

Photographers and Photojournalists

OVERVIEW

Photographers take and sometimes develop and print pictures of people, places, objects, and events, using a variety of cameras and photographic equipment. They work in the publishing, advertising, public relations, science, and business industries, as well as provide personal photographic services. They may also work as fine artists.

Photojournalists shoot photographs that capture news events. Their job is to tell a story with pictures. They may cover a war in central Africa, the Olympics, a national election, or a small town's Fourth of July parade. In addition to shooting pictures, photojournalists also write captions or other supporting text to provide further detail about each photograph. Photojournalists may also develop and print photographs or edit film. There are approximately 130,000 photographers and photojournalists employed in the United States.

HISTORY

The word *photograph* means "to write with light." Although the art of photography goes back only about 150 years, the two Greek words that were chosen and combined to refer to this skill quite accurately describe what it does.

QUICK FACTS

School Subjects
Art
Journalism

Personal Skills
Artistic
Communication/ideas

Work Environment
Indoors and outdoors
Primarily multiple locations

Minimum Education Level
Some postsecondary training

Salary Range
$14,610 to $25,050 to $51,960+

Certification or Licensing
None available

Outlook
About as fast as the average

DOT
131, 143

GOE
01.04.01

NOC
5121, 5221

O*NET-SOC
27-4021.00

The discoveries that led eventually to photography began early in the 18th century when a German scientist, Dr. Johann H. Schultze, experimented with the action of light on certain chemicals. He found that when these chemicals were covered by dark paper they did not change color, but when they were exposed to sunlight, they darkened. A French painter named Louis Daguerre became the first photographer in 1839, using silver-iodide-coated plates and a small box. To develop images on the plates, Daguerre exposed them to mercury vapor. The daguerreotype, as these early photographs came to be known, took minutes to expose and the developing process was directly to the plate. There were no prints made.

Although the daguerreotype was the sensation of its day, it was not until George Eastman invented a simple camera and flexible roll film that photography began to come into widespread use in the late 1800s. After exposing this film to light and developing it with chemicals, the film revealed a color-reversed image, which is called a negative. To make the negative positive (in other words, to print a picture), light must be shone though the negative on to light-sensitive paper. This process can be repeated to make multiple copies of an image from one negative.

Photojournalism started in the early 1920s with the development of new camera equipment that could be easily transported as news occurred. A growing market for photographically illustrated magazines revealed a population wanting news told through pictures and also reflected a relatively low level of literacy among the general public. As World Wars I and II ravaged Europe and the rest of the world, reporters were either handed a camera or were accompanied by photographers to capture the gruesome and sometimes inspirational images of courage during combat.

In 1936, *Life* magazine was launched and quickly became one of the most popular vehicles for the photo essay, a news piece consisting mainly of photographs and their accompanying captions. Soon, however, photojournalists left the illustrated magazine market for news organizations catering to the larger newspapers and television networks. Less emphasis was placed on the photo essay; instead, photojournalists were more often asked to track celebrities or gather photos for newspaper advertising.

One of the most important developments in recent years is digital photography. In digital photography, instead of using film, pictures are recorded on microchips, which can then be downloaded onto a computer's hard drive. They can be manipulated in size, color, and shape, virtually eliminating the need for a darkroom. In the professional world, digital images are primarily used in electronic publishing and advertising since printing technology hasn't quite caught up with camera technology. However, printing technology is also advancing, and even amateur photographers can use digital cameras and home printers to shoot, manipulate, correct, and print snapshots.

Digital photography has also affected the field of photojournalism. Many papers have pared down their photography staff and purchase stock photos from photo agencies. Some smaller papers might even hand staff reporters digital cameras to illustrate their own stories. Still, photojournalists have a place in the working world, as their trained "eyes" for perfect shots will always be in demand.

THE JOB

Photography is both an artistic and technical occupation. There are many variables in the process that a knowledgeable photographer can manipulate to produce a clear image or a more abstract work of fine art. First, all photographers (including photojournalists) know how to use cameras and can adjust focus, shutter speeds, aperture, lenses, and filters. They know about the types and speeds of films. Photographers also know about light and shadow, deciding when to use available natural light and when to set up artificial lighting to achieve desired effects.

Some photographers send their film to laboratories, but others develop their own negatives and make their own prints. These processes require knowledge about chemicals such as developers and fixers and how to use enlarging equipment. Photographers must also be familiar with the large variety of papers available for printing photographs, all of which deliver a different effect. Most photographers continually experiment with photographic processes to improve their technical proficiency or to create special effects.

Digital photography is a relatively new development. With this new technology, film is replaced by microchips that record pictures in digital format. Pictures can then be downloaded onto a computer's hard drive. Photographers use special software to manipulate the images on screen. Digital photography is used primarily for electronic publishing and advertising.

Photographers usually specialize in one of several areas: portraiture, commercial and advertising photography, fine art, educational photography, or scientific photography. There are subspecialties within each of these categories. A *scientific photographer*, for example, may specialize in aerial or underwater photography. A *commercial photographer* may specialize in food or fashion photography.

Another popular specialty for photographers is photojournalism. Photojournalists are photographers who capture stories of everyday life or news events that, supported with words, tell stories to the entire world or to the smallest of communities. Photojournalists are the eyes

Photojournalists often work in dangerous conditions, including wars and scenes of civil strife. *(David Turnley/Corbis)*

of the community, allowing viewers to be a part of events that they would otherwise not have access to.

Actually shooting the photographs is just a portion of what photojournalists do. They also write the cutlines or captions that go with each photograph, develop the film in the darkroom, and edit the film for production. For large photo-essay assignments, they research the subject matter and supervise the layout of the pages. Since most newspapers are now laid out on computers, today's photojournalists download or scan their pictures into a computer and save images on disks.

More often than not, photojournalists use digital cameras to eliminate the need for developing and scanning film. Since the debut of the first digital camera designed for newspapers in the early 1990s, digital photography has revolutionized photojournalism. Unlike traditional film cameras, digital cameras use electronic memory rather than a negative to record an image. The image can then be downloaded instantly into a computer and sent worldwide via email or by posting it on the Internet. By eliminating developing and transportation time, digital cameras enable a sports photographer to shoot a picture of the game-winning basket and immediately transmit it to a newspaper hundreds of miles away before a late-night deadline.

Some photojournalists work on the staffs of weekly or daily newspapers, while others take photographs for magazines or specialty journals. Most magazines employ only a few or no photographic staff, but depend on freelance photojournalists to provide their pictures. Magazine photojournalists sometimes specialize in a specific field, such as sports or food photography.

Some photographers and photojournalists write for trade and technical journals, teach photography in schools and colleges, act as representatives of photographic equipment manufacturers, sell photographic equipment and supplies, produce documentary films, or do freelance work.

REQUIREMENTS

High School

While in high school, take as many art classes and photography classes as are available. Chemistry is useful for understanding developing and printing processes. You can learn about photo manipulation software and digital photography in computer classes, and business classes will help if you are considering a freelance career.

If you decide to specialize in photojournalism, you will need a well-rounded education. Take classes in English, foreign language, history, and the sciences to prepare yourself for the job.

Postsecondary Training

Formal educational requirements depend upon the nature of the photographer's specialty. For instance, photographic work in scientific and engineering research generally requires an engineering background with a degree from a recognized college or institute.

A college education is not required to become a photographer or photojournalist, although college training probably offers the most promising assurance of success in fields such as industrial, news, or scientific photography. There are degree programs at the associate's, bachelor's, and master's levels. Many men and women, however, become photographers with no formal education beyond high school.

Many journalism programs require their students to complete internships with newspapers or other local employers. This is essential to building your experience and getting a good job in this competitive field. Many photojournalists are offered their first jobs directly from their internship experience.

Other Requirements

You should possess manual dexterity, good eyesight and color vision, and artistic ability to succeed in this line of work. You need an eye for form and line, an appreciation of light and shadow, and the ability to use imaginative and creative approaches to photographs or film, especially in commercial work. In addition, you should be patient and accurate and enjoy working with detail.

Self-employed (or freelance) photographers need good business skills. They must be able to manage their own studios, including hiring and managing assistants and other employees, keeping records, and maintaining photographic and business files. Marketing and sales skills are also important to a successful freelance photography business.

Because of the timely nature of many assignments, photojournalists must be able to work under the pressures of a deadline. They may be assigned to shoot pictures of people in trying situations, such as house fires, car wrecks, or military combat. In these cases, the photojournalist must be extremely sensitive to the people at the center of the story, ask permission to take photos, and when possible, ask for details about what happened. To do this, photojournalists must be extremely tactful and polite and work well under stress.

EXPLORING

Photography is a field that anyone with a camera can explore. To learn more about this career, you can join high school camera clubs, yearbook or newspaper staffs, photography contests, and community hobby groups. You can also seek a part-time or summer job in a camera shop or work as a developer in a laboratory or processing center.

EMPLOYERS

About 130,000 photographers and photojournalists work in the United States, more than half of whom are self-employed. Most jobs for photographers are provided by photographic or commercial art studios; other employers include newspapers and magazines, radio and TV broadcasting, government agencies, and manufacturing firms. Colleges, universities, and other educational institutions employ photographers to prepare promotional and educational materials.

A large percentage of photojournalists work as freelance contractors. Photo agencies and news organizations such as the Associated Press purchase photos from freelance photojournalists to use in print and online publications. Some photojournalists work on staff for newspapers, magazines, or other print publications. Television networks also hire photojournalists to help illustrate breaking stories.

STARTING OUT

Some photographers enter the field as apprentices, trainees, or assistants. Trainees may work in a darkroom, camera shop, or developing laboratory. They may move lights and arrange backgrounds for a commercial or portrait photographer. Assistants spend many months learning this kind of work before they move into a job behind a camera.

Many large cities offer schools of photography, which may be a good way to start in the field. Beginning photojournalists may work for one of the many newspapers and magazines published in their area. Other photographers choose to go into business for themselves as soon as they have finished their formal education. Setting up a studio may not require a large capital outlay, but beginners may find that success does not come easily.

ADVANCEMENT

Because photography is such a diversified field, there is no usual way in which to get ahead. Those who begin by working for someone else may advance to owning their own businesses. Commercial photographers may gain prestige as more of their pictures are placed in well-known trade journals or popular magazines. Photojournalists can advance by shooting for more prestigious papers (and earning more money for it) or by going into business on their own. They can advance to become the head photo editor, in charge of a staff of photojournalists, or they can even become managing editors or editors in chief of a publication. Other newspaper photojournalists move into magazine photography, usually on a freelance basis. Where newspaper photojournalists are generalists, magazine photography is usually more specific in nature. A few photographers may become celebrities in their own right by making contributions to the art world or the sciences.

EARNINGS

The U.S. Department of Labor reports that salaried photographers earned median annual salaries of $25,050 in 2003. Salaries ranged from less than $14,610 to more than $51,960. Photographers earned the following mean annual salaries in 2003 by industry: newspaper, book, and directory publishers, $36,670; radio and television broadcasting, $31,380; and colleges and universities, $33,380.

Self-employed photographers often earn more than salaried photographers, but their earnings depend on general business conditions.

In addition, self-employed photographers do not receive the benefits that a company provides its employees.

Photographers in salaried jobs usually receive benefits such as paid holidays, vacations, and sick leave and medical insurance.

WORK ENVIRONMENT

Work conditions vary based on the job and employer. Many photographers work a 35- to 40-hour workweek, but freelancers and news photographers often put in long, irregular hours. Commercial and portrait photographers work in comfortable surroundings. Photojournalists seldom are assured physical comfort in their work and may in fact face danger when covering stories on natural disasters or military conflicts. Some photographers work in research laboratory settings; others work on aircraft; and still others work underwater. For some photographers, conditions change from day to day. One day, they may be photographing a hot and dusty rodeo; the next they may be taking pictures of a dog sled race in Alaska.

In general, photographers work under pressure to meet deadlines and satisfy customers. Freelance photographers have the added pressure of uncertain incomes and have to continually seek out new clients.

For freelance photographers, the cost of equipment can be quite expensive, with no assurance that the money spent will be repaid through income from future assignments. Freelancers in travel-related photography, such as travel and tourism photographers and photojournalists, have the added cost of transportation and accommodations. For all photographers, flexibility is a major asset.

OUTLOOK

Employment of photographers and photojournalists will increase about as fast as the average for all occupations through 2012, according to the *Occupational Outlook Handbook*. The demand for new images should remain strong in education, communication, entertainment, marketing, and research. As the Internet grows and more newspapers and magazines turn to electronic publishing, demand will increase for photographers to produce digital images.

Photography is a highly competitive field. There are far more photographers and photojournalists than positions available. Only those who are extremely talented and highly skilled can support themselves as self-employed workers in these professions. Many photographers and photojournalists take pictures as a sideline while working another job.

FOR MORE INFORMATION

The ASMP promotes the rights of photographers and photojournalists, educates its members in business practices, and promotes high standards of ethics.

American Society of Media Photographers (ASMP)
150 North Second Street
Philadelphia, PA 19106
Tel: 215-451-2767
http://www.asmp.org

The NPPA maintains a job bank, provides educational information, and makes insurance available to its members. It also publishes News Photographer *magazine.*

National Press Photographers Association (NPPA)
3200 Croasdaile Drive, Suite 306
Durham, NC 27705
Tel: 919-383-7246
Email: info@nppa.org
http://www.nppa.org

This organization provides training, publishes its own magazine, and offers various services for its members.

Professional Photographers of America
229 Peachtree Street, NE, Suite 2200
Atlanta, GA 30303
Tel: 800-786-6277
Email: csc@ppa.com
http://www.ppa.com

For information on student membership, contact
Student Photographic Society
229 Peachtree Street, NE, Suite 2200
Atlanta, GA 30303
Tel: 800-339-5325
Email: info@studentphoto.com
http://www.studentphoto.com

Prepress Workers

QUICK FACTS

School Subjects
Computer science
Mathematics
Technical/shop

Personal Skills
Artistic
Technical/scientific

Work Environment
Primarily indoors
Primarily one location

Minimum Education Level
Some postsecondary training

Salary Range
$18,390 to $31,660 to
$51,260+

Certification or Licensing
Voluntary

Outlook
Decline

DOT
979

GOE
08.03.05

NOC
9472

O*NET-SOC
51-5021.00, 51-5022.00,
51-5022.01, 51-5022.02,
51-5022.03, 51-5022.04,
51-5022.05, 51-5022.06,
51-5022.07, 51-5022.08

OVERVIEW

Prepress workers handle the first stage in the printing process. This initial phase of production involves multiple steps, including creating pages from text and graphics and making printing plates. With the introduction of desktop publishing and other computer technology, the prepress process has changed dramatically over the past decade. Computerized processes have replaced many of the traditional processes, eliminating a number of prepress jobs but opening up new opportunities as well.

According to the U.S. Department of Labor, 148,000 people are employed in prepress jobs. Approximately 56,000 of these jobs are with commercial printing companies. Other jobs are with prepress service bureaus (companies that deal exclusively with prepress work) and newspapers.

HISTORY

The history of modern printing began with the invention of movable type in the 15th century. For several centuries before that, books had been printed from carved wooden blocks or laboriously copied by hand. These painstaking methods of production were so expensive that books were chained to prevent theft.

In the 1440s, Johannes Gutenberg invented a form of metal type that could be used over and over. The first known book to be printed with this movable type was a Bible in 1455—the now-famous Gutenberg Bible. Gutenberg's revolutionary new type greatly reduced the time and cost involved in printing, and books soon became plentiful.

Ottmar Mergenthaler, a German immigrant to the United States, invented the Linotype machine in 1886. Linotype allowed the typesetter to set type from a keyboard that used a mechanical device to set letters in place. Before this, printers were setting type by hand, one letter at a time, picking up each letter individually from their typecases as they had been doing for more than 400 years. At about the same time, Tolbert Lanston invented the Monotype machine, which also had a keyboard but set the type as individual letters. These inventions allowed compositors to set type much faster and more efficiently.

With these machines, newspapers advanced from the small two-page weeklies of the 1700s to the huge editions of today's metropolitan dailies. The volume of other periodicals, advertisements, books, and other printed matter also proliferated.

In the 1950s, a new system called photocomposition was introduced into commercial typesetting operations. In this system, typesetting machines used photographic images of letters, which were projected onto a photosensitive surface to compose pages. Instructions to the typesetting machine about which letters to project and where to project them were fed in through a punched-paper or magnetic tape, which was, in turn, created by an operator at a keyboard.

Most recently, typesetting has come into the home and office in the form of desktop publishing. This process has revolutionized the industry by enabling companies and individuals to do their own type composition and graphic design work.

THE JOB

Prepress work involves a variety of tasks, most of which are now computer-based. The prepress process is typically broken down into the following areas of responsibility: compositor and typesetter, paste-up worker, desktop publishing specialist, pre-flight technician, output technician, scanner operator, camera operator, lithographic artist, film stripper, and platemaker.

Compositors and *typesetters* are responsible for setting up and arranging type by hand or by computer into galleys for printing. This is done using "cold type" technology (as opposed to the old "hot type" method, which involved using molten lead to create letters and lines of text). A common method is phototypesetting, in which type is entered into a computer and output on photographic film or paper. Typesetting in its traditional sense requires a *paste-up worker* to then position illustrations and lay out columns of type. This manual process is quickly being phased out by desktop publishing.

Most often today, desktop publishing is the first step in the production process. The *desktop publisher* designs and lays out text and graphics on a personal computer according to the specifications of the job. This involves sizing text, setting column widths, and arranging copy with photos and other images. All elements of the piece are displayed on the computer screen and manipulated using a keyboard and mouse. In commercial printing plants, jobs tend to come from customers on computer disk, eliminating the need for initial desktop publishing work on the part of the printing company. (For more information, see the article Desktop Publishing Specialists)

The entire electronic file is reviewed by the *pre-flight technician* to ensure that all of its elements are properly formatted and set up. At small print shops—which account for the majority of the printing industry—a *job printer* is often the person in charge of typesetting, page layout, proofing copy, and fixing problems with files.

Once a file is ready, the *output technician* transmits it through an imagesetter onto paper, film, or directly to a plate. The latter method is called digital imaging, and it bypasses the film stage altogether. Direct-to-plate technology has been adopted by only a small percentage of printing companies nationwide, but it is expected to be universal within the next decade.

If a file is output onto paper or provided camera-ready, the *camera operator* photographs the material and develops film negatives, either by hand or by machine. Because the bulk of commercial printing today is done using lithography, most camera operators can also be called *lithographic photographers.*

Often it is necessary to make corrections, change or reshape images, or lighten or darken the film negatives. This is the job of the *lithographic artist,* who, depending on the area of specialty, might have the title *dot etcher, retoucher,* or *letterer.* This film retouching work is highly specialized and is all done by hand using chemicals, dyes, and special tools.

The *film stripper* is the person who cuts film negatives to the proper size and arranges them onto large sheets called flats. The pieces are taped into place so that they are in proper position for the plate to be made.

The *platemaker,* also called a *lithographer* because of the process used in most commercial plants, creates the printing plates. This is done using a photographic process. The film is laid on top of a thin metal plate treated with a light-sensitive chemical. It is exposed to ultraviolet light, which "burns" the positive image into the plate.

Those areas are then chemically treated so that when ink is applied to the plate, it adheres to the images to be printed and is repelled by the non-printing areas.

Lithography work traditionally involved sketching designs on stone, clay, or glass. Some of these older methods are still used for specialized purposes, but the predominant method today is the one previously described, which is used in offset printing. In offset printing, a series of cylinders are used to transfer ink from the chemically treated plate onto a rubber cylinder (called a blanket), then onto the paper. The printing plate never touches the paper but is "offset" by the rubber blanket.

If photos and art are not provided electronically, the *scanner operator* scans them using a high-resolution drum or flatbed scanner. In the scanning process, the continuous color tone of the original image is interpreted electronically and converted into a combination of the four primary colors used in printing: cyan (blue), magenta, yellow, and black—commonly called CMYK. A screening process separates the image into the four colors, each of which is represented by a series of dots called a halftone. These halftones are recorded to film, from which printing plates are made. During the printing process, ink applied to each of the plates combines on paper to recreate the color of the original image.

REQUIREMENTS

Educational requirements for prepress workers vary according to the area of responsibility, but all require at least a high school diploma, and most call for a strong command of computers.

Whereas prepress areas used to be typesetting and hand-composition operations run by people skilled in particular crafts, they are now predominantly computer-based. Workers are no longer quite as specialized and generally are competent in a variety of tasks. Thus, one of the most important criteria for prepress workers today is a solid base of computer knowledge, ideally in programs and processes related to graphic design and prepress work.

High School

Young people interested in the field are advised to take courses in computer science, mathematics, and electronics.

Postsecondary Training

The more traditional jobs, such as camera operator, film stripper, lithographic artist, and platemaker, require longer, more specialized preparation. This might involve an apprenticeship or a two-year associate's degree. But these jobs now are on the decline as they are replaced by computerized processes.

Postsecondary education is strongly encouraged for most prepress positions and a requirement for some jobs, including any managerial role. Graphic arts programs are offered by community and junior colleges as well as four-year colleges and universities. Postsecondary programs in printing technology are also available.

Any programs or courses that give you exposure to the printing field will be an asset. Courses in printing are often available at vocational-technical institutes and through printing trade associations.

Certification or Licensing

The National Council for Skill Standards in Graphic Communications has established a list of competencies for workers in the printing industry. To demonstrate their knowledge, operators can take examinations in composition, job engineering, image capture, and digital output. Applicants receive the expert digital imaging technician designation for each examination that they successfully complete. Applicants who complete all four examinations are awarded the designation, master digital imaging technician.

Other Requirements

Prepress work requires strong communications skills, attention to detail, and the ability to perform well in a high-pressure, deadline-driven environment. Physically, you should have good manual dexterity, good eyesight, and good overall visual perception. Artistic skill is an advantage in nearly any prepress job.

EXPLORING

A summer job or internship doing basic word processing or desktop publishing is one way to get a feel for what prepress work involves. Such an opportunity could even be found through a temporary agency. Of course, you will need a knowledge of computers and certain software.

You also can volunteer to do desktop publishing or design work for your school newspaper or yearbook. This would have the added benefit of exposing you to the actual printing process.

EMPLOYERS

Most prepress work is in firms that do commercial or business printing and in newspaper plants. Other jobs are at companies that specialize in certain aspects of the prepress process, for example, platemaking or outputting of film.

Because printing is so widespread, prepress jobs are available in almost any part of the country. However, according to the *Occupational Outlook Handbook,* prepress work is concentrated in large printing centers like New York, Chicago, Los Angeles, Philadelphia, Dallas, and Washington, D.C.

STARTING OUT

Information on apprenticeships and training opportunities is available through state employment services and local chapters of printing industry associations.

If you wish to start working first and learn your skills on the job you should contact potential employers directly, especially if you want to work in a small nonunion print shop. Openings for trainee positions may be listed in newspaper want ads or with the state employment service. Trade school graduates may find jobs through their school's placement office. And industry association offices often run job-listing services.

ADVANCEMENT

Some prepress work, such as typesetting, can be learned fairly quickly; other jobs, like film stripping or platemaking, take years to master. Workers often begin as assistants and move into on-the-job training programs. Entry-level workers are trained by more experienced workers and advance according to how quickly they learn and prove themselves.

In larger companies, prepress workers can move up the ranks to take on supervisory roles. Prepress and production work is also a good starting point for people who aim to become a customer service or sales representative for a printing company.

EARNINGS

Pay rates vary for prepress workers, depending on their level of experience and responsibility, type of company, where they live, and whether or not they are union members. Prepress technicians and workers had median annual earnings of $31,660 in 2003. Salaries ranged from less than $18,390 to $51,260 or more. Mean earnings in commercial printing, the industry employing the largest number of prepress technicians and workers, were $34,950.

WORK ENVIRONMENT

Generally, prepress workers work in clean, quiet settings away from the noise and activity of the pressroom. Prepress areas are usually air-conditioned and roomy. Desktop publishers and others who work in front of computer terminals can risk straining their eyes, as well as their backs and necks. Film stripping and other detail-oriented work also can be tiring to the eyes. The chemicals used in platemaking can irritate the skin.

An eight-hour day is typical for most prepress jobs, but frequently workers put in more than eight hours. Prepress jobs at newspapers and financial printers often call for weekend and evening hours.

OUTLOOK

Overall employment in the prepress portion of the printing industry is expected to decline through 2012, according to the U.S. Department of Labor. While it is anticipated that the demand for printed materials will increase, prepress work will not, mainly because of new innovations.

Almost all prepress operations are computerized, and many of the traditional jobs that involved highly skilled hand work—film strippers, paste-up workers, photoengravers, camera operators, and platemakers—are being phased out. The computer-oriented aspects of prepress work have replaced most of these tasks. Employment of desktop publishing specialists, however, is expected to grow faster than the average. Demand for preflight technicians will also be strong. And specialized computer skills will increasingly be needed to handle direct-to-plate and other new technology.

Given the increasing demand for rush print jobs, printing trade service companies should offer good opportunities for prepress workers. Larger companies and companies not equipped for specialized prepress work will continue to turn to these specialty shops to keep up with their workload.

FOR MORE INFORMATION

This organization offers information, services, and training related to printing, electronic prepress, electronic publishing, and other areas of the graphic arts industry.

Graphic Arts Information Network
Graphic Arts Technical Foundation/Printing Industries of America
200 Deer Run Road
Sewickley, PA 15143-2600

Tel: 412-741-6860
Email: info@gatf.org
http://www.gain.net/PIA_GATF/learning_center/prepress.html

This organization represents U.S. and Canadian workers in all craft and skill areas of the printing and publishing industries. In addition to developing cooperative relationships with employers, it also offers education and training through local union schools.
Graphic Communications International Union
1900 L Street, NW
Washington, DC 20036
Tel: 202-462-1400
http://www.gciu.org

This trade association of graphic communications and graphic arts supplier companies offers economic and management information, publications, and industry reports and studies.
IPA-The Association of Graphic Solutions Providers
7200 France Avenue South, Suite 223
Edina, MN 55435
Tel: 800-255-8141
Email: info@ipa.org
http://www.ipa.org

This graphic arts trade association is a good source of general information.
National Association for Printing Leadership
75 West Century Road
Paramus, NJ 07652-1408
Tel: 800-642-6275
Email: Information@napl.org
http://public.napl.org

For information on careers and educational institutions, visit
Graphic Comm Central
http://teched.vt.edu/gcc

Printing Press Operators and Assistants

QUICK FACTS

School Subjects
Computer science
Mathematics
Technical/shop

Personal Skills
Mechanical/manipulative
Technical/scientific

Work Environment
Primarily indoors
Primarily one location

Minimum Education Level
High school diploma

Salary Range
$17,440 to $29,340 to
$46,830+

Certification or Licensing
Voluntary

Outlook
More slowly than the average

DOT
651

GOE
08.03.05

NOC
7381

O*NET-SOC
51-5023.09

OVERVIEW

Printing press operators and *printing press operator assistants* prepare, operate, and maintain printing presses. Their principal duties include installing and adjusting printing plates, loading and feeding paper, mixing inks and controlling ink flow, and ensuring the quality of the final printed piece.

There are approximately 199,000 printing press operators in the United States. They are mostly employed by newspaper plants and commercial and business printers.

HISTORY

The forerunners of today's modern printing presses were developed in Germany in the 15th century. They made use of the new concept of movable type, an invention generally credited to Johannes Gutenberg. Before Gutenberg's time, most books were copied by hand or printed from carved wooden blocks. Movable type used separate pieces of metal that could be easily set in place, locked into a form for printing, and then used again for another job.

The first presses consisted of two flat surfaces. Once set in place, the type was inked with a roller, and a sheet of paper was pressed against the type with a lever. Two people working together could print about 300 pages a day.

In the early 19th century, Friedrich Konig, another German, developed the first cylinder press. With a cylinder press, the paper is mounted on a large cylinder that is rolled over a flat printing surface.

The first rotary press was developed in the United States in 1865 by William Bullock. On this kind of press, the inked surface is on a revolving cylinder called a plate cylinder. The plate cylinder acts like a roller and prints onto a continuous sheet of paper (called a web) coming off a giant roll.

The speed and economy of the web press was improved by the discovery of offset printing in the early 20th century. In this process, the raised metal type used in earlier processes was substituted with a flexible plate that could be easily attached to the plate cylinder. The ink is transferred from the plate onto a rubber cylinder (called a blanket) and then onto the paper. The printing plate never touches the paper but is "offset" by the rubber blanket.

Offset printing uses the process of lithography, in which the plate is chemically treated so that ink sticks only to the parts that are to be printed and is repelled by the non-print areas.

Offset lithography is the most common form of printing today and is used on both web-fed and sheet-fed presses. Web-fed presses are used for newspapers and other large-volume, lower-cost runs. The fastest web presses today can print about 150,000 complete newspapers in an hour. Sheet-fed presses, which print on single sheets of paper rather than a continuous roll, are used for smaller, higher-quality jobs.

Other forms of printing are gravure (in which depressions on an etched plate are inked and pressed to paper), flexography (a form of rotary printing using flexible rubber plates with raised image areas and fast-drying inks), and letterpress (the most traditional method, in which a plate with raised, inked images is pressed against paper).

THE JOB

The duties of press operators and their assistants vary according to the size of the printing plant in which they work. Generally, they are involved in all aspects of making the presses ready for a job and monitoring and operating the presses during the print run. Because most presses now are computerized, the work of press operators involves both electronic and manual processes.

In small shops, press operators usually handle all of the tasks associated with running a press, including cleaning and oiling the parts and making minor repairs. In larger shops, press operators are aided by assistants who handle most maintenance and cleanup tasks.

Once the press has been inspected and the printing plate arrives from the platemaker, the "makeready" process begins. In this stage, the operators mount the plates into place on the printing surface or cylinder. They mix and match the ink, fill the ink fountains, and adjust the ink flow and dampening systems. They also load the paper, adjust the press to the paper size, feed the paper through the cylinders and, on a web press, adjust the tension controls. When this is done, a proof sheet is run off for the customer's review.

When the proof has been approved and final adjustments have been made, the press run begins. During the run, press operators constantly check the quality of the printed sheets and make any necessary adjustments. They look to see that the print is clear and properly positioned and that ink is not offsetting (blotting) onto other sheets. If the job involves color, they make sure that the colors line up properly with the images they are assigned to (registration). Operators also monitor the chemical properties of the ink and correct temperatures in the drying chamber, if the press has one.

On a web press, the feeding and tension mechanisms must be continually monitored. If the paper tears or jams, it must be rethreaded. As a roll of paper runs out, a new one must be spliced onto the old one. According to the book *Careers in Graphic Communications* by Sally Ann Flecker and Pamela J. Groff (Graphic Arts Technical Foundation, 1998), some web presses today can print up to 50,000 feet an hour. At this rate, the press might run through a giant roll of paper every half hour. In large web printing plants, it takes an entire crew of specialized operators to oversee the process.

Most printing plants now have computerized printing presses equipped with sophisticated instrumentation. Press operators work at a control panel that monitors the printing processes and can adjust each variable automatically.

REQUIREMENTS

High School
The minimum educational requirement for printing press operators and assistants is a high school diploma. Students interested in this field should take courses that offer an introduction to printing and color theory, as well as chemistry, computer science, electronics, mathematics, and physics—any course that develops mechanical and mathematical aptitude.

Postsecondary Training
Traditionally, press operators learned their craft through apprenticeship programs ranging from four to five years. Apprenticeships are

A printing press operator checks a page for quality during the printing process. *(R. R. Donnelley & Sons)*

still available, but they are being phased out by postsecondary programs in printing equipment operation offered by technical and trade schools and community and junior colleges. Information on apprenticeships is often available through state employment services and local chapters of printing industry associations. Additionally, many press operators and assistants still receive informal on-the-job training after a printer hires them.

Computer training is also essential to be successful in the printing industry today. With today's rapid advances in technology, "students need all the computer knowledge they can get," advises John Smotherman, press operator and shift supervisor at Busch and Schmidt Company in Broadview, Illinois.

Certification or Licensing
The National Council for Skill Standards in Graphic Communications has established a list of competencies—what an operator should know and be able to do—for the expert level of performance. Skill standards are available for electronic imaging, sheetfed and web offset press, flexographic press, and finishing and distribution. Operators can take an examination in flexographic press operation, sheet fed press operation, or web press operation to receive the designation of national council certified operator.

Other Requirements

Strong communication skills, both verbal and written, are a must for press operators and assistants. They also must be able to work well as a team, both with each other and with others in the printing company. Any miscommunication during the printing process can be costly if it means re-running a job or any part of it. Working well under pressure is another requirement because most print jobs run on tight deadlines.

EXPLORING

High school is a good time to begin exploring the occupation of printing press operator. Some schools offer print shop classes, which provide the most direct exposure to this work. Working on the high school newspaper or yearbook is another way to gain a familiarity with the printing process. A delivery job with a print shop or a visit to a local printing plant will offer you the chance to see presses in action and get a feel for the environment in which press operators work. You also might consider a part-time, temporary, or summer job as a cleanup worker or press feeder in a printing plant.

EMPLOYERS

There are approximately 199,000 press operators employed in the United States. The bulk of these work for newspapers and commercial and business printers. Companies range from small print shops, where one or two press operators handle everything, to large corporations that employ teams of press operators to work around the clock.

Other press operator jobs are with in-plant operations, that is, in companies and organizations that do their own printing in-house.

Because printing is so geographically diverse, press operator jobs are available in almost any city or town in the country. However, according to the *Occupational Outlook Handbook*, press work is concentrated in large printing centers like New York, Chicago, Los Angeles, Philadelphia, Dallas, and Washington, D.C.

STARTING OUT

Openings for trainee positions may be listed in newspaper want ads or with the state employment service. Trade school graduates may find jobs through their school's placement office. And industry association offices often run job listing services.

John Smotherman notes that many young people entering the field start out in a part-time position while still in school. "I think students should pursue all the classroom education they can, but many intricacies of the printing process, like how certain inks and papers work together, need to be learned through experience," he says.

ADVANCEMENT

Most printing press operators, even those with some training, begin their careers doing entry-level work, such as loading, unloading, and cleaning the presses. In large print shops, the line of promotion is usually as follows: press helper, press assistant, press operator, press operator-in-charge, press room supervisor, superintendent.

Press operators can advance in salary and responsibility level by learning to work more complex printing equipment, for example, by moving from a one-color press to a four-color press. Printing press operators should be prepared to continue their training and education throughout their careers. As printing companies upgrade their equipment and buy new, more computerized presses, retraining will be essential.

Press operators who are interested in other aspects of the printing business also may find advancement opportunities elsewhere in their company. Those with business savvy may be successful in establishing their own print shops.

EARNINGS

Pay rates vary for press operators, depending on their level of experience and responsibility, type of company, where they live, and whether or not they are union members. Median annual earnings of press operators were $29,340 in 2003, according to the U.S. Department of Labor (USDL). Salaries ranged from less than $17,440 to $46,830 or more. The USDL reports the following annual mean earnings for printing press operators by industry: printing and related support activities, $32,770; converted paper product manufacturing, $32,280; and advertising and related services, $26,840.

WORK ENVIRONMENT

Pressrooms are well ventilated, well lit, and humidity controlled. They are also noisy. Often press operators must wear ear protectors. Press work can be physically strenuous and requires a lot of standing. Press operators also have considerable contact with ink and cleaning fluids that can cause skin and eye irritation.

Working around large machines can be hazardous, so press operators must constantly observe good safety habits.

An eight-hour day is typical for most press operators, but some work longer hours. Smaller plants generally have only a day shift, but many larger plants and newspaper printers run around the clock. At these plants, like in hospitals and factories, press operator shifts are broken into day, afternoon/evening, and "graveyard" hours.

OUTLOOK

The U.S. Department of Labor predicts that employment of press operators will grow more slowly than the average through 2012. An increased demand for printed materials—advertising, direct mail pieces, computer software packaging, books, and magazines—will be offset by the use of larger, more efficient machines. Additionally, new business practices such as printing-on-demand (where materials are printed in smaller amounts as they are requested by customers instead of being printed in large runs that may not be used) and electronic publishing (which is the publication of materials on the Internet or through other electronic methods of dissemination) will also limit opportunities for workers in this field.

Newcomers to the field are likely to encounter stiff competition from experienced workers or workers who have completed retraining programs to update their skills. Opportunities are expected to be greatest for students who have completed formal apprenticeships or postsecondary training programs.

FOR MORE INFORMATION

This organization offers information, services, and training related to printing, electronic prepress, electronic publishing, and other areas of the graphic arts industry.

Graphic Arts Information Network
Graphic Arts Technical Foundation/Printing Industries of America
200 Deer Run Road
Sewickley, PA 15143-2600
Tel: 412-741-6860

Email: info@gatf.org
http://www.gain.net

This organization represents U.S. and Canadian workers in all craft and skill areas of the printing and publishing industries. In addition to developing cooperative relationships with employers, it also offers education and training through local union schools.

Graphic Communications International Union
1900 L Street, NW
Washington, DC 20036
Tel: 202-462-1400
http://www.gciu.org

This trade association of graphic communications and graphic arts supplier companies offers economic and management information, publications, and industry reports and studies.

**IPA-The Association of Graphic Solutions
   Providers**
7200 France Avenue South, Suite 223
Edina, MN 55435
Tel: 800-255-8141
Email: info@ipa.org
http://www.ipa.org

This graphic arts trade association is a good source of general information.

National Association for Printing Leadership
75 West Century Road
Paramus, NJ 07652-1408
Tel: 800-642-6275
Email: Information@napl.org
http://public.napl.org

For more information on the national council certified operator designation, contact

**National Council for Skill Standards in Graphic
   Communications**
Harry V. Quadracci Printing & Graphic Center
800 Main Street
Pewaukee, WI 53072
Tel: 262-695-3470
Email: ekelley@ncssgc.org
http://www.ncssgc.org

For information on careers and educational institutions, visit
Graphic Comm Central
http://teched.vt.edu/gcc

Reporters

OVERVIEW

Reporters are the foot soldiers for newspapers, magazines, and television and radio broadcast companies. They gather and analyze information about current events and write stories for publication or for broadcasting. News analysts, reporters, and correspondents hold approximately 66,000 jobs in the United States.

HISTORY

Newspapers are some of the primary disseminators of news in the United States. People read newspapers to learn about the current events that are shaping their society and societies around the world. Newspapers give public expression to opinion and criticism of government and societal issues, and, of course, provide the public with entertaining, informative reading.

Newspapers are able to fulfill these functions because of the freedom given to the press. However, this was not always the case. The first American newspaper, published in 1690, was suppressed four days after it was published. And it was not until 1704 that the first continuous newspaper appeared.

One early newspaperman who later became a famous writer was Benjamin Franklin. Franklin worked for his brother at a Boston newspaper before publishing his own paper two years later in 1723 in Philadelphia.

A number of developments in the printing industry made it possible for newspapers to be printed more cheaply. In the late 19th century, new types of presses were developed to increase production, and more importantly, the Linotype machine was invented. The Linotype

QUICK FACTS

School Subjects
English
Journalism

Personal Skills
Communication/ideas
Helping/teaching

Work Environment
Indoors and outdoors
Primarily multiple locations

Minimum Education Level
Bachelor's degree

Salary Range
$17,900 to $31,240 to $75,149+

Certification or Licensing
None available

Outlook
More slowly than the average

DOT
131

GOE
01.03.01

NOC
5123

O*NET-SOC
27-3020.00, 27-3021.00, 27-3022.00

mechanically set letters so that handset type was no longer necessary. This dramatically decreased the amount of prepress time needed to get a page into print. Newspapers could respond to breaking stories more quickly, and late editions with breaking stories became part of the news world.

These technological advances, along with an increasing population, factored into the rapid growth of the newspaper industry in the United States. In 1776, there were only 37 newspapers in the United States. Today there are more than 1,500 daily and nearly 7,500 weekly newspapers in the country.

As newspapers grew in size and widened the scope of their coverage, it became necessary to increase the number of employees and to assign them specialized jobs. Reporters have always been the heart of newspaper staffs. However, in today's complex world, with the public hungry for news as it occurs, reporters and correspondents are involved in all media—not only newspapers, but magazines, radio, and television as well. Today, with the advent of the Internet, many newspapers are going online, creating many opportunities for reporting on the Web.

THE JOB

Reporters collect information on newsworthy events and prepare stories for newspaper or magazine publication or for radio or television broadcast. The stories may simply provide information about local, state, or national events, or they may present opposing points of view on issues of current interest. In this latter capacity, the press plays an important role in monitoring the actions of public officials and others in positions of power.

Stories may originate as an assignment from an editor or as the result of a lead or news tip. Good reporters are always on the lookout for good story ideas. To cover a story, they gather and verify facts by interviewing people involved in or related to the event, examining documents and public records, observing events as they happen, and researching relevant background information. Reporters generally take notes or use a tape recorder as they collect information and write their stories once they return to their offices. In order to meet a deadline, they may have to telephone the stories to *rewriters,* who write or transcribe the stories for them. After the facts have been gathered and verified, the reporters transcribe their notes, organize their material, and determine what emphasis, or angle, to give the news. The story is then written to meet prescribed standards of editorial style and format.

The basic functions of reporters are to observe events objectively and impartially, record them accurately, and explain what the news means in a larger, societal context. Within this framework, there are several types of reporters.

The most basic is the *news reporter*. This job sometimes involves covering a beat, which means that the reporter may be assigned to consistently cover news from an area such as the local courthouse, police station, or school system. It may involve receiving general assignments, such as a story about an unusual occurrence or an obituary of a community leader. Large daily papers may assign teams of reporters to investigate social, economic, or political events and conditions.

Many newspaper, wire service, and magazine reporters specialize in one type of story, either because they have a particular interest in the subject or because they have acquired the expertise to analyze and interpret news in that particular area. *Topical reporters* cover stories for a specific department, such as medicine, politics, foreign affairs, sports, consumer affairs, finance, science, business, education, labor, or religion. They sometimes write features explaining the history that has led up to certain events in the field they cover. *Feature writers* generally write longer, broader stories than news reporters, usually on more upbeat subjects, such as fashion, art, theater, travel, and social events. They may write about trends, for example, or profile local celebrities. *Editorial writers* and *syndicated news columnists* present viewpoints that, although based on a thorough knowledge, are opinions on topics of popular interest. *Columnists* write under a byline and usually specialize in a particular subject such as politics or government activities. *Critics* review restaurants, books, works of art, movies, plays, musical performances, and other cultural events.

Specializing allows reporters to focus their efforts, talent, and knowledge on one area of expertise. It also gives them more opportunities to develop deeper relationships with contacts and sources, which is necessary to gain access to the news.

Correspondents report events in locations distant from their home offices. They may report news by mail, telephone, fax, or computer from rural areas, large cities throughout the United States, or countries. Many large newspapers, magazines, and broadcast companies have one correspondent who is responsible for covering all the news for the foreign city or country where they are based. These reporters are known as *foreign correspondents*.

Reporters on small or weekly newspapers not only cover all aspects of the news in their communities, but also may take photographs, write editorials and headlines, lay out pages, edit wire-service copy,

Reporters interview Secretary of Defense Donald Rumsfeld during an informal press conference in Mazar-e-Sharif, Afghanistan. *(U.S. Department of Defense)*

and help with general office work. *Television reporters* may have to be photogenic as well as talented and resourceful; they may at times present live reports, filmed by a mobile camera unit at the scene where the news originates, or they may tape interviews and narration for later broadcast.

REQUIREMENTS

High School
High school courses that will provide you with a firm foundation for a reporting career include English, journalism, history, social studies, communications, typing, and computer science. Speech courses will help you hone your interviewing skills, which are necessary for success as a reporter. In addition, it will be helpful to take college prep courses, such as foreign language, math, and science.

Postsecondary Training
You will need at least a bachelor's degree to become a reporter, and a graduate degree will give you a great advantage over those entering the field with lesser degrees. Most editors prefer applicants with degrees in journalism because their studies include liberal arts courses as well as professional training in journalism. Some editors consider it sufficient for a reporter to have a good general education from a liberal arts college. Others prefer applicants with an undergradu-

ate degree in liberal arts and a master's degree in journalism. The great majority of journalism graduates hired today by newspapers, wire services, and magazines have majored specifically in news-editorial journalism.

More than 400 colleges offer programs in journalism leading to a bachelor's degree. In these schools, around three-fourths of a student's time is devoted to a liberal arts education and one-fourth to the professional study of journalism, with required courses such as introductory mass media, basic reporting and copy editing, history of journalism, and press law and ethics. Students are encouraged to select other journalism courses according to their specific interests.

Journalism courses and programs are also offered by many community and junior colleges. Graduates of these programs are prepared to go to work directly as general assignment reporters, but they may encounter difficulty when competing with graduates of four-year programs. Credit earned in community and junior colleges may be transferable to four-year programs in journalism at other colleges and universities. Journalism training may also be obtained in the armed forces. Names and addresses of newspapers and a list of journalism schools and departments are published in the annual *Editor & Publisher International Year Book: The Encyclopedia of the Newspaper Industry* (New York: Editor & Publisher) which is available for reference in most public libraries and newspaper offices.

A master's degree in journalism may be earned at approximately 120 schools, and a doctorate at about 35 schools. Graduate degrees may prepare students specifically for careers in news or as journalism teachers, researchers, and theorists, or for jobs in advertising or public relations.

A reporter's liberal arts training should include courses in English (with an emphasis on writing), sociology, political science, economics, history, psychology, business, speech, and computer science. Knowledge of foreign languages is also useful. To be a reporter in a specialized field, such as science or finance, requires concentrated course work in that area.

Other Requirements

In order to succeed as a reporter, it is crucial that you have typing skill, as you will type your stories using word processing programs. Although not essential, a knowledge of shorthand or speedwriting makes note taking easier, and an acquaintance with news photography is an asset.

Median Annual Earnings for Bachelor's Degree Recipients in Journalism and Mass Communications, 2003

Type of Employer	Salary
Web-based companies	$32,000
Cable television	$28,000
Public relations	$28,000
Newsletters, trades	$27,000
Advertising	$27,000
Daily newspapers	$25,000
Consumer magazines	$25,000
Weekly newspapers	$24,000
Radio	$24,000
Television	$22,000
All employers	$26,000

Source: University of Georgia, Grady College of Journalism and Mass Communication, Annual Survey of Journalism & Mass Communications Graduates, 2003

You must also be inquisitive, aggressive, persistent, and detail-oriented. You should enjoy interaction with people of various races, cultures, religions, economic levels, and social statuses.

EXPLORING

You can explore a career as a reporter in a number of ways. You can talk to reporters and editors at local newspapers and radio and TV stations. You can interview the admissions counselor at the school of journalism closest to your home.

In addition to taking courses in English, journalism, social studies, speech, computer science, and typing, high school students can acquire practical experience by working on school newspapers or on a church, synagogue, or mosque newsletter. Part-time and summer jobs on newspapers provide invaluable experience to the aspiring reporter.

College students can develop their reporting skills in the laboratory courses or workshops that are part of the journalism curriculum.

College students might also accept jobs as campus correspondents for selected newspapers. People who work as part-time reporters covering news in a particular area of a community are known as *stringers* and are paid only for those stories that are printed.

More than 3,000 journalism scholarships, fellowships, and assistantships are offered by universities, newspapers, foundations, and professional organizations to college students. Many newspapers and magazines offer summer internships to journalism students to provide them with practical experience in a variety of basic reporting and editing duties. Students who successfully complete internships are usually placed in jobs more quickly upon graduation than those without such experience.

EMPLOYERS

Of the approximately 66,000 reporters and correspondents employed in the United States, approximately 60 percent work for newspaper, periodical, book, and directory publishers. About 25 percent work in radio and television broadcasting. The rest are employed by wire services.

STARTING OUT

Jobs in this field may be obtained through college placement offices or by applying directly to the personnel departments of individual employers. If you have some practical experience, you will have an advantage; you should be prepared to present a portfolio of material you wrote as a volunteer or part-time reporter, or other writing samples.

Most journalism school graduates start out as general assignment reporters or copy editors for small publications. A few outstanding journalism graduates may be hired by large city newspapers or national magazines. They are trained on the job. But they are the exception, as large employers usually require several years' experience. As a rule, novice reporters cover routine assignments, such as reporting on civic and club meetings, writing obituaries, or summarizing speeches. As you become more skilled in reporting, you will be assigned to more important events or to a regular beat, or you may specialize in a particular field.

ADVANCEMENT

Reporters may advance by moving to larger newspapers or press services, but competition for such positions is unusually keen. Many highly qualified reporters apply for these jobs every year.

A select number of reporters eventually become columnists, correspondents, editorial writers, editors, or top executives. These important and influential positions represent the top of the field, and competition is strong for them.

Many reporters transfer the contacts and knowledge developed in newspaper reporting to related fields, such as public relations, advertising, or preparing copy for radio and television news programs.

EARNINGS

There are great variations in the earnings of reporters. Salaries are related to experience, the type of employer for which the reporter works, geographic location, and whether the reporter is covered by a contract negotiated by the Newspaper Guild.

According to the U.S. Department of Labor, the median salary for news analysts, reporters, and correspondents was $31,240 in 2003. The lowest paid 10 percent of these workers earned $17,900 or less per year, while the highest paid 10 percent made $71,520 or more annually.

According to the Newspaper Guild, the average top minimum salary for reporters with about five years' experience was $44,586 in 2003. Salaries range from $20,150 to $75,149 or more.

The U.S. Department of Labor reported that reporters and correspondents who worked in radio and television broadcasting had mean annual earnings of $48,450 in 2003.

WORK ENVIRONMENT

Reporters work under a great deal of pressure in settings that differ from the typical business office. Their jobs generally require a five-day, 35- to 40-hour week, but overtime and irregular schedules are very common. Reporters employed by morning papers start work in the late afternoon and finish around midnight, while those on afternoon or evening papers start early in the morning and work until early or mid-afternoon. Foreign correspondents often work late at night to send the news to their papers in time to meet printing deadlines.

The day of the smoky, ink-stained newsroom has passed, but newspaper offices are still hectic places. Reporters have to work amid the clatter of computer keyboards and other machines, loud voices engaged in telephone conversations, and the bustle created by people hurrying about. An atmosphere of excitement prevails, especially as press deadlines approach.

Travel is often required in this occupation, and assignments such as covering wars, political uprisings, fires, floods, and other events of a volatile nature may be dangerous.

OUTLOOK

Employment for reporters and correspondents through 2012 is expected to grow more slowly than the average for all occupations, according to the *Occupational Outlook Handbook*. While the number of self-employed reporters and correspondents is expected to grow, newspaper jobs are expected to decrease because of mergers, consolidations, and closures in the newspaper industry.

Because of an increase in the number of small community and suburban daily and weekly newspapers, opportunities will be best for journalism graduates who are willing to relocate and accept relatively low starting salaries. With experience, reporters on these small papers can move up to editing positions or may choose to transfer to reporting jobs on larger newspapers or magazines.

Openings will be limited on big city dailies. While individual papers may enlarge their reporting staffs, little or no change is expected in the total number of these newspapers. Applicants will face strong competition for jobs on large metropolitan newspapers. Experience is a definite requirement, which rules out most new graduates unless they possess credentials in an area for which the publication has a pressing need. Occasionally, a beginner can use contacts and experience gained through internship programs and summer jobs to obtain a reporting job immediately after graduation.

A significant number of jobs will be provided by magazines and in radio and television broadcasting, but the major news magazines and larger broadcasting stations generally prefer experienced reporters. For beginning correspondents, small stations with local news broadcasts will continue to replace staff who move on to larger stations or leave the business. Network hiring has been cut drastically in the past few years and will probably continue to decline. Stronger employment growth is expected for reporters in online newspapers and magazines.

Overall, the prospects are best for graduates who have majored in news-editorial journalism and completed an internship while in school. The top graduates in an accredited program will have a great advantage, as will talented technical and scientific writers. Small newspapers prefer to hire beginning reporters who are acquainted with the community and are willing to help with photography and other aspects of production. Without at least a bachelor's degree in journalism, applicants will find it increasingly difficult to obtain even an entry-level position.

Those with doctorates and practical reporting experience may find teaching positions at four-year colleges and universities, while highly qualified reporters with master's degrees may obtain employment in journalism departments of community and junior colleges.

Poor economic conditions do not drastically affect the employment of reporters and correspondents. Their numbers are not severely cut back even during a downturn; instead, employers forced to reduce expenditures will suspend new hiring.

FOR MORE INFORMATION

For a list of accredited programs in journalism and mass communications, visit the ACEJMC website:

Accrediting Council on Education in Journalism and Mass
    Communications (ACEJMC)
University of Kansas School of Journalism
    and Mass Communications
Stauffer-Flint Hall, 1435 Jayhawk Boulevard
Lawrence, KS 66045-7575
http://www.ku.edu/~acejmc/STUDENT/PROGLIST.SHTML

This organization provides general educational information on all areas of journalism, including newspapers, magazines, television, and radio.

Association for Education in Journalism and Mass
    Communication
234 Outlet Pointe Boulevard
Columbia, SC 29210-5667
Tel: 803-798-0271
Email: aejmchq@aejmc.org
http://www.aejmc.org

To read The Journalist's Road to Success: A Career Guide, *which lists schools offering degrees in news-editing, and financial aid to those interested in print journalism, visit the DJNF website:*

Dow Jones Newspaper Fund
PO Box 300
Princeton, NJ 08543-0300
Tel: 609-452-2820
Email: newsfund@wsj.dowjones.com
http://djnewspaperfund.dowjones.com/fund

For information on careers in newspapers and industry facts and figures, contact
Newspaper Association of America
1921 Gallows Road, Suite 600
Vienna, VA 22182-3900
Tel: 703-902-1600
Email: IRC@naa.org
http://www.naa.org

For information on union membership, contact
Newspaper Guild-Communication Workers of America
501 Third Street, NW, Suite 250
Washington, DC 20001
Tel: 202-434-7177
Email: guild@cwa-union.org
http://www.newsguild.org

Visit the following website for comprehensive information on journalism careers, summer programs, and college journalism programs:
High School Journalism
http://www.highschooljournalism.org

For comprehensive information for citizens, students, and news people about the field of journalism, visit
Project for Excellence in Journalism and the Committee of Concerned Journalists
http://www.journalism.org

Sportswriters

QUICK FACTS

School Subjects
English
Journalism
Physical education

Personal Skills
Communication/ideas

Work Environment
Indoors and outdoors
Primarily multiple locations

Minimum Education Level
Bachelor's degree

Salary Range
$22,090 to $42,330 to
$87,390+

Certification or Licensing
None available

Outlook
About as fast as the average

DOT
131

GOE
01.03.01

NOC
5231

O*NET-SOC
27-3022.00

OVERVIEW

Sportswriters cover the news in sports for newspapers and magazines. They research original ideas or follow up on breaking stories, contacting coaches, athletes, and team owners and managers for comments or more information. Sometimes a sportswriter is fortunate enough to get his or her own column, in which the sportswriter editorializes on current news or developments in sports.

HISTORY

Throughout the world there are some 7,200 daily newspapers and far more semiweeklies, biweeklies, and weeklies, circulating at least 500 million copies on a regular basis. In the international context, the average newspaper is crude, poorly printed, heavy with sensational news, light on serious criticism, and burdened by all types of problems (especially economic). Outside Western Europe and North America there are very few "elite," or ultra serious, newspapers. Although most of the world's newspapers are privately owned, some degree of government control is evident in many countries.

Magazine journalism has been a potent force in the United States (and throughout the world), appealing mainly to the elite, the well educated, and the opinion leaders. At least this is true in the sense of "journalistic" magazines. Generally more incisive, more articulate, more interpretive, and certainly more comprehensive than newspapers, magazines have supplied an important intellectual dimension to news-oriented journalism. Whereas the main function of newspaper journalism is to inform or summarize in brief fashion, the aim of most magazine journalism is to fill gaps—

to explain, interpret, criticize, and comment. In short, magazine journalism in its many types and styles supplements newspapers and fleshes out the bare bones of newspaper journalism.

Most magazines and newspapers have sections that focus on sports; others, such as *Sports Illustrated* and *ESPN the Magazine,* focus entirely on sports reporting. In either case, sportswriters are needed to write articles about athletes, teams, and sports competitions. Sportswriters are employed by both newspapers and magazines throughout the United States.

THE JOB

The sportswriter's primary job is to report the outcomes of the sports events that occurred that day. Since one newspaper can't employ enough reporters to cover, in person, every single high school, college, and professional sports event that happens on any given day, let alone sports events happening in other cities and countries, sportswriters use the wire news services to get the details. Major national and international wire services include Reuters, AP, UPI, Agence France-Presse, and ITAR-TASS. The entire body of statistics for tennis matches, hockey games, and track-and-field events, for example, can be sent over the wire service so that sportswriters can include the general story and the vital statistics in as condensed or lengthy a form as space allows.

A sportswriter begins work each day by reviewing the local, national, and international news that comes in over the wire news services. He or she then begins researching the top or lead stories to try to flesh out the story, perhaps with a local perspective on it, or to come up with a new angle or spin altogether. An example of a lead story might be the comeback of a professional tennis star; the underdog victory of a third-rate, much-maligned football team; the incredible pitching record of a high school athlete; or the details about a football running back who blew out his knee in a crucial last-minute play. The sportswriter then calls or interviews in person coaches, athletes, scouts, agents, promoters, and sometimes, in the case of an athletic injury, a physician or team of physicians.

Depending on the edition of the newspaper or magazine, the sportswriter might report events that happened anywhere from the day before to events that took place within that week or month. For example, a sportswriter who writes for a magazine such as *Sports Illustrated* probably won't write articles with the same degree of detail per game. Instead, he or she writes articles, commonly called *features,* that explore an entire season for a team or an athlete. The magazine sportswriter might take the same story of the running back with the damaged knee ligaments and follow that athlete through his surgery and rehabilitation, interviewing not only the running back, but his wife, doctors, coaches, and agent. This stage of gathering information is the same for both newspaper and magazine sportswriters, the only difference is the time line; a newspaper sportswriter may have only a few hours to conduct research and call around for comments, while the sportswriter for a magazine may have anywhere from several weeks to several months to compose the story.

Regardless of whether the sportswriter works for a newspaper or magazine, the next step for the sportswriter is to write the story. The method will vary, again, depending on the medium. Most sportswriters for newspapers are subject to the constraints of space, and these limits can change in a matter of minutes. On a dull day, up until the hour before the paper is published (or *put to bed*), the sportswriter might have a quarter of a page to fill with local sports news. At the last minute, however, an entire Super Bowl team could come down with food poisoning, in which case the sports editor would probably want to cover this larger, breaking story. To accommodate the new articles about the poisoning, the effect on team morale, whether or not the Super Bowl might be postponed for the first time in history, the local sports coverage would either have to shrink considerably or be completely cut. To manage this, sportswriters, like other reporters who write for daily newspapers, compose their stories with the most crucial facts contained within the first one or two paragraphs of the story. They may write a 10-paragraph story, but if it had to be shortened, the pertinent information would be easily retained.

Sportswriters for magazines, on the other hand, seldom need to worry about their stories being cut down at the last minute. Rather, their stories are subject to more careful editing. Magazines usually have story meetings weeks or months in advance of the relevant issue, giving sportswriters ample time to plan, research, and write their articles. As a result of the different timetable, the presentation of the story will change. The sportswriter will not cram all the essential facts into an opening paragraph or two. Instead, he or she is allowed much greater leeway with the introduction and the rest of the article. The sportswriter, in this case, will want to set a mood in the introduction, developing the characters of the individuals being interviewed—literally, telling a story about the story. In short, details can hinder a newspaper sports story from accomplishing its goal of getting across the facts in a concise form, while in a magazine sports article, those extraneous, revealing details actually become part of the story.

Books to Read

Bailey-Hughes, Brenda. *The Administrative Assistant.* Menlo Park, Calif.: Crisp Publications, 1997.

Brown, Gerry, and Mike Morrison, eds. *ESPN Sports Almanac 2005: The Definitive Sports Reference Book.* New York: Hyperion, 2004.

Ferguson, Donald L. *Opportunities in Journalism Careers.* New York: McGraw-Hill/Contemporary Books, 2001.

Fink, Conrad C. *Sportswriting: The Lively Game.* Ames, Iowa: Iowa State Press/Blackwell Publishing Company, 2001.

Russo, Christopher, and Allen St. John. *The Mad Dog 100: The Greatest Sports Arguments of All Time.* New York: Doubleday, 2003.

Stout, Glenn, ed. *The Best American Sports Writing 2004.* Boston: Houghton Mifflin Company, 2004.

Even with the help of news services, sportswriters still couldn't have all the sports news at their fingertips without the help of other reporters and writers, known in the world of reporting as *stringers.* A stringer covers an event that, most likely, would not be covered by the wire services, such as high school sports events, as well as games in professional sports that are occurring simultaneously with other major sports events. The stringer attends the sports event and phones in scores, or emails or faxes in a complete report.

While the sportswriters for magazines don't necessarily special-ize in one area of sports, but instead, routinely write features on a wide variety of sports and athletes, sportswriters for newspapers do specialize. Many only cover a particular sport, such as baseball. Others are assigned a beat, or specific area, and like other reporters must cover all the events that fall into that beat. For example, a sportswriter assigned to the high school football beat for a news-paper in Los Angeles, California, would be expected to cover all the area high school football games. Since football is seasonal, he or she might be assigned to the high school basketball beat during the winter season. On the other hand, the sportswriter working in Lexington, Kentucky, might be assigned coverage of all the high school sports in the area, not simply one sport. Much of the way in which assignments are given depends on experience as well as budget and staffing constraints.

REQUIREMENTS

High School

English, journalism, and speech are the most important classes for you to take in high school. You will need to master the art of writing in order to be able to convey your ideas concisely, yet creatively, to your readers. Speech classes will help you become comfortable interacting with others. Be sure to take physical education classes and participate in organized sports, be it as a competitor, a team manager, or an assistant. You also should join the staff of your school paper or yearbook. This will give you a chance to cover and write about your school's sports teams or other school activities.

Postsecondary Training

You will need at least a bachelor's degree to become a sportswriter, although many sportswriters go on to study journalism at the graduate level. Most sportswriters concentrate on journalism while in college, either by attending a program in journalism or by taking whatever courses are available outside of a specialized program. This isn't to say that you can't become a sportswriter without a degree in journalism, but competition for sportswriting jobs is incredibly fierce. After all, sportswriters get great seats at sports events, and they have the credentials to get them into interviews with sports celebrities. Increasingly, a specialized education is becoming the means by which sports editors and managers sift through the stacks of resumes from prospective sportswriters. Sportswriters may have degrees in communications or English, among other majors.

Other Requirements

Clearly, the ability to write well and concisely is another requirement for the job of the sportswriter. In addition, you must have a solid understanding of the rules and play of many different sports. If you hope to specialize in the coverage of one particular sport, your knowledge of that sport has to be equal to that of anyone coaching or playing it at the professional level.

Finally, you must be able to elicit information from a variety of sources, as well as to determine when information being leaked is closer to promotional spin than to fact. There will be more times when a coach or agent will not want to comment on a story than the times when they will want to make an on-the-record comment, so the sportswriter must be assertive in pressing the source for more information.

EXPLORING

You can learn on-the-job skills by working for your high school and college papers. The experience can be related to sports, of course, but any journalistic experience will help you develop the basic skills useful to any reporter, regardless of the area about which you are writing.

You can increase your chances and success in the field by applying to colleges or universities with renowned academic programs in journalism. Most accredited programs have a required period of training in which you will intern with a major newspaper somewhere in the United States; student-interns are responsible for covering a beat.

You may also find it helpful to read publications that are related to this field, such as *Sports Illustrated* (http://www.si.com) and *Sports Business Journal* (http://www.sportsbusinessjournal.com), and visit websites such as the Associated Press Sports Editors (http://apse.dallasnews.com).

EMPLOYERS

Sportswriters are employed by newspapers and magazines throughout the world. They may cover professional teams based in large cities or high school teams located in tiny towns. Sportswriters also work as freelance writers.

STARTING OUT

You may have to begin your career as a sportswriter by covering the games or matches that no else wants to or can cover. As a stringer, you won't earn much money, you'll probably have a second or even third job, but eventually it may lead to covering bigger and better games and teams. Some sportswriters make a living out of covering sports for very small towns, others only work at those jobs until they have gained the experience to move on.

Most journalists start their careers by working in small markets— little towns and cities with local papers. You may work for a newspaper for a year or two and then apply for positions with larger papers in bigger towns and cities. Sportswriters for newspapers follow the same routine, and more than a few end up pursuing areas other than sports because the job openings in sports simply weren't there. The lucky few who hang on to a small sports beat can often parlay that beat into a better position by sticking with the job and demonstrating a devotion to the sport, even cultivating a following of loyal fans. This could lead to a full-time column.

Most likely, as a sportswriter, you will take advantage of opportunities to learn more about athletes and sports in general. Becoming an expert on a little known but rapidly growing sport may be one way for you to do this. For example, if you were to learn all that you can about mountain biking, you might be able to land a job with one of the magazines specializing in the sport of mountain biking.

Competition for full-time jobs with magazines as a sportswriter is just as keen as it is for major newspapers. Often, a sportswriter will write articles and try to sell them to one of the major magazines, hoping that when an opening comes, he or she will have first crack at it. Still, most sportswriters move into the world of sports magazines after they've proven themselves in newspaper sportswriting. It is possible, however, to get a job with a sports magazine straight from college or graduate school; chances are, you'll have to work your way up, though.

The placement centers of colleges or universities with accredited undergraduate and graduate programs in journalism can be extremely helpful in beginning your job search. In fact, many graduates of these programs are not only highly sought after by newspapers and magazines, but these graduates are often offered jobs by the newspapers and magazines with whom they had an internship during school.

ADVANCEMENT

The constraints of budget, staffing, and time—which make a sportswriters' job difficult—are also often what can help a sportswriter rise through the ranks. For example, the writer asked to cover all the sports in a small area may have to hustle to cover the beat alone, but that writer also won't have any competition when covering the big events. Thus, he or she can gain valuable experience and bylines writing for a small paper, whereas in a larger market, the same sportswriter would have to wait much longer to be assigned an event that might result in a coveted byline.

Sportswriters advance by gaining the top assignments, covering the major sports in feature articles, as opposed to the bare bones summaries of events. They also advance by moving to larger and larger papers, by getting columns, and finally, by getting a syndicated column—that is, a column carried by many papers around the country or even around the world.

Sportswriters for magazines advance by moving up the publishing ladder, from editorial assistant to associate editor to writer. Often, an editorial assistant might be assigned to research a story for a sports brief—a quirky or short look at an element of the game. For example, *Sports Illustrated* might have a page devoted to new advances in sports equipment for the amateur athlete. The editorial assistant might be given the idea and asked to research it, or specific items. A writer might eventually write it up, using the editorial assistant's notes. Advancement, then, comes in being actually listed as the author of the piece.

In the publishing worlds of both newspapers and magazines, sportswriters can advance by becoming editors of a newspaper's sports page or of a sports magazine. There are also *sports publicists* and *sports information directors* who work for the publicity and promotions arms of colleges, universities, and professional sports teams. These individuals release statements, write and disseminate to the press articles on the organizations' teams and athletes, and arrange press opportunities for coaches and athletes.

EARNINGS

According the U.S. Department of Labor, writers earned median annual earnings of $42,330 in 2003. The lowest 10 percent earned less than $22,090, while the highest 10 percent earned $87,390 or more. The median annual salary for all writers in the newspaper and book publishing industries was $43,040.

Sportswriters who cover the major sports events, who have their own column, or who have a syndicated column can expect to earn more than the salaries above. Sportswriters who write for major magazines can also expect to earn more, sometimes per article, depending on their reputations and the contracts worked out by themselves or their agents.

WORK ENVIRONMENT

Like other journalists, sportswriters work in a variety of conditions, from the air-conditioned offices of a newsroom or magazine publisher to the sweaty, humid locker room of a professional basketball team, to the arid and dusty field where a baseball team's spring training is held. Sportswriters work irregular hours, putting in as much or as little time as the story requires, often traveling to small towns and out-of-the-way locales to cover a team's away games.

The benefits are obvious—for the individuals who love sports, the job offers the chance to cover sports events every day; to immerse themselves in the statistics and injury lists and bidding wars of professional and amateur sports; to speak, sometimes one-on-one, with the greatest athletes of yesterday, today, and tomorrow.

OUTLOOK

The turnover rate for top sportswriters with major newspapers and magazines isn't very high, which means that job openings occur as sportswriters retire, die, are fired, or move into other markets. While the publishing industry may have room in it for yet another magazine devoted to a particular sports specialty, competition for sportswriting jobs will continue to be strong through 2012 and beyond.

FOR MORE INFORMATION

Founded in 1958 by the Wall Street Journal *to improve the quality of journalism education, this organization offers internships, scholarships, and literature for college students. To read* The Journalist's Road to Success: A Career Guide, *which lists schools offering degrees in news-editing, and financial aid to those interested in print journalism, visit the DJNF website.*

Dow Jones Newspaper Fund
PO Box 300
Princeton, NJ 08543-0300
Tel: 609-452-2820
Email: newsfund@wsj.dowjones.com
http://djnewspaperfund.dowjones.com/fund

Career information, including a pamphlet called Facts about Newspapers, *is available from*
Newspaper Association of America
1921 Gallows Road, Suite 600
Vienna, VA 22182-3900
Tel: 703-902-1600
http://www.naa.org

For information on careers and salaries in the newspaper industry, contact
The Newspaper Guild
501 Third Street, NW, Suite 250
Washington, DC 20001

Tel: 202-434-7177
Email: guild@cwa-union.org
http://www.newsguild.org

This organization for journalists has campus and online chapters.
Society of Professional Journalists
Eugene S. Pulliam National Journalism Center
3909 North Meridian Street
Indianapolis, IN 46208
Tel: 317-927-8000
Email: questions@spj.org
http://spj.org

Visit the following website for comprehensive information on journalism careers, summer programs, and college journalism programs.
High School Journalism
http://www.highschooljournalism.org

Writers

QUICK FACTS

School Subjects
English
Journalism

Personal Skills
Communication/ideas
Helping/teaching

Work Environment
Primarily indoors
Primarily one location

Minimum Education Level
Bachelor's degree

Salary Range
$22,090 to $42,330 to
$87,390+

Certification or Licensing
None available

Outlook
About as fast as the average

DOT
131

GOE
01.02.01

NOC
5121

O*NET-SOC
27-3043.00

OVERVIEW

Journalistic *writers* express, edit, promote, and interpret ideas and facts in written form for newspapers, magazines, books, websites, and radio and television broadcasts. There are approximately 139,000 salaried writers in the United States.

HISTORY

The skill of writing has existed for thousands of years. Papyrus fragments with writing by ancient Egyptians date from about 3000 B.C., and archaeological findings show that the Chinese had developed books by about 1300 B.C. A number of technical obstacles had to be overcome before printing and the profession of writing evolved. Books of the Middle Ages were copied by hand on parchment. The ornate style that marked these books helped ensure their rarity. Also, few people were able to read. Religious fervor prohibited the reproduction of secular literature.

The development of the printing press by Johannes Gutenberg in the middle of the 15th century and the liberalism of the Protestant Reformation, which helped encourage a wider range of publications, greater literacy, and the creation of a number of works of literary merit, helped develop the publishing industry. The first authors worked directly with printers.

The modern publishing age began in the 18th century. Printing became mechanized, and the novel, magazine, and newspaper developed. The first newspaper in the American colonies appeared in the early 18th century, but it was Benjamin Franklin who, as editor and writer, made the *Pennsylvania Gazette* one of the most influential in setting a high standard for his fellow American journalists. Franklin also published the first magazine in the colonies, *The American Magazine,* in 1741.

Advances in the printing trades, photoengraving, retailing, and the availability of capital produced a boom in newspapers and magazines in the 19th century. Further mechanization in the printing field, such as the use of the Linotype machine, high-speed rotary presses, and special color reproduction processes, set the stage for still further growth in the book, newspaper, and magazine industry.

In addition to the print media, the broadcasting industry has contributed to the development of the professional writer. Radio, television, and the Internet are sources of information, education, and entertainment that provide employment for thousands of journalistic writers.

THE JOB

Journalistic writers deal with the written word, whether it is destined for the printed page, broadcast, or computer screen. The nature of their work is as varied as the materials they produce: newspapers, magazines, books, content for websites, and scripts for radio and television broadcast. Writers develop ideas and write for all media.

Staff writers are employed by magazines and newspapers to write news stories, feature articles, and columns about a wide variety of subjects including politics, government, education, entertainment, sports, science, health, food, consumer affairs, and local, regional, or national news. First they come up with an idea for an article from their own interests or are assigned a topic by an editor. The topic is of relevance to the particular publication; for example, a writer for a magazine on entertainment may be assigned an article on the Academy Awards. Then writers begin gathering as much information as possible about the subject through library research, interviews, the Internet, observation, and other methods. They keep extensive notes from which they will draw material for their project. Once the material has been organized and arranged in logical sequence, writers prepare a written outline. The process of developing a piece of writing is exciting, although it can also involve detailed and solitary work. After researching an idea, a writer might discover that a different perspective or related topic would be more effective, entertaining, or marketable.

Columnists or *commentators* analyze news and social issues. They write about events from the standpoint of their own experience or opinion.

Editorial writers write on topics of public interest, and their comments, consistent with the viewpoints and policies of their employers, are intended to stimulate or mold public opinion.

Foreign correspondents report on news from countries outside of where their newspapers or magazines are located. Other foreign correspondents work for radio or television networks.

Critics review restaurants, books, works of art, movies, plays, musical performances, and other cultural events.

Newswriters work for radio or TV news departments writing news stories, news "teases," special features, investigative reports, and entire newscasts, which include news, weathercasts, sportscasts, traffic reports, and other broadcast content. They do this by researching and fact checking information obtained from reporters, news wires, press releases, research, and telephone and email interviews. Newswriters must be able to write clear, concise stories that fit in a specific allotted time period. Newswriters employed in television broadcasting must be able to match the words they write with the images that are broadcast to help illustrate the story. Since most radio and television stations broadcast 24 hours a day, newswriters are needed to work daytime, evening, and overnight shifts.

When working on assignment, writers usually submit their outlines to an editor or other company representative for approval. Then they write a first draft, trying to put the material into words that will have the desired effect on their audience. They often rewrite or polish sections of the material as they proceed, always searching for just the right way of imparting information or expressing an idea or opinion. A manuscript may be reviewed, corrected, and revised numerous times before a final copy is submitted. Even after that, an editor may request additional changes.

Writers for newspapers, magazines, or books often specialize in their subject matter. Some writers might have an educational background that allows them to give critical interpretations or analyses. For example, a health or science writer for a newspaper typically has a degree in biology and can interpret new ideas in the field for the average reader.

Writers can be employed either as in-house staff or as freelancers. Pay varies according to experience and the position, but freelancers must provide their own office space and equipment such as computers and fax machines. Freelancers also are responsible for keeping tax records, sending out invoices, negotiating contracts, and providing their own health insurance.

Top Daily Newspapers in the United States

1. *USA Today*
2. *Wall Street Journal*
3. *New York Times*
4. *Los Angeles Times*
5. *Washington Post*
6. *New York Daily News*
7. *Chicago Tribune*
8. *New York Post*
9. *New York Newsday*
10. *Houston Chronicle*

Notes: By circulation as of September 30, 2002

Source: Editor & Publisher International Year Book 2003

REQUIREMENTS

High School

While in high school, build a broad educational foundation by taking courses in English, literature, foreign languages, history, general science, social studies, computer science, and typing. The ability to type is almost a requisite for many positions in the journalism field, as is familiarity with computers.

Postsecondary Training

Competition for journalistic writing jobs almost always demands the background of a college education. Many employers prefer you have a broad liberal arts background or majors in English, literature, history, philosophy, or one of the social sciences. Other employers desire communications or journalism training in college. Occasionally a master's degree in a specialized writing field may be required. A number of schools offer courses in journalism, and some of them offer courses or majors in newspaper and magazine writing, publication management, book publishing, and writing for the Internet.

In addition to formal course work, most employers look for practical writing experience. If you have worked on high school or college newspapers, yearbooks, or literary magazines, you will make a better candidate, as well as if you have worked for small community newspapers or radio stations, even in an unpaid position. Many magazines, newspapers, and radio and television stations have summer internship programs that provide valuable training if you want to learn about the publishing and broadcasting businesses. Interns do many simple tasks, such as running errands and answering phones, but some may be asked to perform research, conduct interviews, or even write some minor pieces.

Other Requirements

To be a journalistic writer, you should be creative and able to express ideas clearly, have a broad general knowledge, be skilled in research techniques, and be computer literate. Other assets include curiosity, persistence, initiative, resourcefulness, and an accurate memory. For some jobs—on a newspaper or a television newsroom, for example, where the activity is hectic and deadlines are short—the ability to concentrate and produce under pressure is essential.

EXPLORING

As a high school or college student, you can test your interest and aptitude in the field of writing by serving as a reporter or writer on school newspapers, yearbooks, and literary magazines. Various writing courses and workshops will offer you the opportunity to sharpen your writing skills.

Small community newspapers and local radio stations often welcome contributions from outside sources, although they may not have the resources to pay for them. Jobs in bookstores, magazine shops, and even newsstands will offer you a chance to become familiar with various publications.

You can also obtain information on writing as a career by visiting local newspapers, publishers, or radio and television stations and interviewing some of the writers who work there. Career conferences and other guidance programs frequently include speakers on the entire field of journalism from local or national organizations.

EMPLOYERS

There are approximately 139,000 writers and authors in the United States. More than one-half of salaried writers and editors work for newspapers, magazines, and book publishers; radio and television broadcasting companies; and Internet publishing and broadcasting companies. Outside the field of journalism, writers are also employed by advertising agencies, public relations firms, and for journals and newsletters published by business and nonprofit organizations, such as professional associations, labor unions, and religious organizations. Other non-journalism employers are government agencies and film production companies. Other writers work as novelists, short story writers, poets, playwrights, and screenwriters.

The major newspaper, magazine, and book publishers and broadcasting companies account for the concentration of journalistic writers in large cities such as New York, Chicago, Los Angeles, Boston, Philadelphia, San Francisco, and Washington, D.C. Opportunities with small publishers and broadcasting companies can be found throughout the country.

STARTING OUT

A fair amount of experience is required to gain a high-level position in the field. Most writers start out in entry-level positions. These jobs may be listed with college career services offices, or they may be obtained by applying directly to the employment departments of the individual publishers or broadcasting companies. Graduates who previously served internships with these companies often have the advantage of knowing someone who can give them a personal recommendation. Want ads in newspapers and trade journals are another source for jobs. Because of the competition for positions, however, few vacancies are listed with public or private employment agencies.

Employers in the field of journalism usually are interested in samples of published writing. These are often assembled in an organized portfolio or scrapbook. Bylined or signed articles are more credible (and, as a result, more useful) than stories whose source is not identified.

Beginning positions as a junior writer usually involve library research, preparation of rough drafts for part or all of a report, cataloging, and other related writing tasks. These are generally carried on under the supervision of a senior writer.

ADVANCEMENT

Most writers find their first jobs as editorial, production, or research assistants. Advancement may be more rapid in small media companies, where beginners learn by doing a little bit of everything and may be given writing tasks immediately. At large publishers or broadcast companies, duties are usually more compartmentalized. Assistants in entry-level positions are assigned such tasks as research and fact checking, but it generally takes much longer to advance to full-scale writing duties.

Promotion into higher-level positions may come with the assignment of more important articles and stories to write, or it may be the result of moving to another company. Mobility among employees in this field is common. A staff writer at one magazine publisher may switch to a similar position at a more prestigious publication. Or a newswriter may switch to a related field as a type of advancement.

Freelance or self-employed writers earn advancement in the form of larger fees as they gain exposure and establish their reputations.

EARNINGS

In 2003, median earnings for all salaried writers were $42,330 a year, according to the U.S. Department of Labor. The lowest 10 percent earned less than $22,090, while the highest 10 percent earned $87,390 or more. Writers employed by newspaper and book publishers had annual mean earnings of $43,040, while those employed in radio and television broadcasting earned $40,130.

In addition to their salaries, many writers earn some income from freelance work. Part-time freelancers may earn from $5,000 to $15,000 a year. Freelance earnings vary widely. Full-time established freelance writers may earn $75,000 or more a year.

WORK ENVIRONMENT

Working conditions vary for journalistic writers. Although their workweek usually runs 35 to 40 hours, many writers work overtime. A publication that is issued frequently has more deadlines closer together, creating greater pressures to meet them. The work is especially hectic on newspapers and at broadcasting companies that operate seven days a week. Writers often work nights and weekends to meet deadlines or to cover a late-developing story.

Most writers work independently, but they often must cooperate with editors, artists, photographers, and rewriters who may have widely differing ideas of how the materials should be prepared and presented.

Physical surroundings range from comfortable private offices to noisy, crowded newsrooms filled with other workers typing and talking on the telephone. Some writers must confine their research to the library or telephone interviews, but others may travel to other cities or countries or to local sites, such as theaters, ballparks, airports, factories, or other offices.

The work is arduous, but most writers are seldom bored. Some jobs, such as that of the foreign correspondent, require travel. The most difficult element is the continual pressure of deadlines. People who are the most content as writers enjoy and work well with deadline pressure.

OUTLOOK

The employment of all writers is expected to increase about as fast as the average rate of all occupations through 2012, according to the U.S. Department of Labor. The demand for writers by newspapers, periodicals, and book publishers is expected to increase. The growth of online publishing on company websites and other online services will also demand many talented writers; those with computer skills will be at an advantage as a result. Employment for all positions in the radio and television broadcasting industry is expected to increase about 9 percent, more slowly than the average for all other occupations through 2012, according to the U.S. Department of Labor.

People entering this field should realize that the competition for jobs is extremely keen. Beginners, especially, may have difficulty finding employment. Of the thousands who graduate each year with degrees in English, journalism, communications, and the liberal arts, intending to establish a career as a writer, many turn to other occupations when they find that applicants far outnumber the job openings available. College students would do well to keep this in mind and prepare for an unrelated alternate career in the event they are unable to obtain a position as writer; another benefit of this approach is that, at the same time, they will become qualified as writers in a specialized field. The practicality of preparing for alternate careers is borne out by the fact that opportunities are best in firms that prepare business and trade publications and in technical writing.

Potential writers who end up working in a field other than journalism may be able to earn some income as freelancers, selling articles, stories, books, and possibly TV and movie scripts, but it is usually difficult for anyone to be self-supporting entirely on independent writing.

FOR MORE INFORMATION

For a list of accredited programs in journalism and mass communications, visit the ACEJMC website.

    **Accrediting Council on Education in Journalism and Mass
       Communications (ACEJMC)**
    University of Kansas School of Journalism and
       Mass Communications

Stauffer-Flint Hall, 1435 Jayhawk Boulevard
Lawrence, KS 66045-7575
http://www.ku.edu/~acejmc/STUDENT/PROGLIST.
SHTML

*This organization provides general educational information on all
areas of journalism, including newspapers, magazines, television,
and radio.*
**Association for Education in Journalism and Mass
    Communication**
234 Outlet Pointe Boulevard
Columbia, SC 29210-5667
Tel: 803-798-0271
Email: aejmchq@aejmc.org
http://www.aejmc.org

*For a list of schools offering degrees in broadcasting as well as schol-
arship information, contact*
Broadcast Education Association
1771 N Street, NW
Washington, DC 20036-2891
Tel: 888-380-7222
Email: beainfo@beaweb.org
http://www.beaweb.org

For information on investigative journalism, contact
Investigative Reporters and Editors
138 Neff Annex
Missouri School of Journalism
Columbia, MO 65211
Tel: 573-882-2042
Email: info@ire.org
http://www.ire.org

The MPA is a good source of information about internships.
Magazine Publishers of America (MPA)
810 Seventh Avenue, 24th Floor
New York, NY 10019
Tel: 212-872-3700
Email: mpa@magazine.org
http://www.magazine.org

For college programs and union information, contact
National Association of Broadcast Employees and Technicians
501 Third Street, NW, 8th Floor
Washington, DC 20001
Tel: 202-434-1254
Email: nabet@nabetcwa.org
http://nabetcwa.org

For broadcast education and scholarship information, contact
National Association of Broadcasters
1771 N Street, NW
Washington, DC 20036
Tel: 202-429-5300
Email: nab@nab.org
http://www.nab.org

For information on writing and editing careers in the field of communications, contact
National Association of Science Writers
PO Box 890
Hedgesville, WV 25427
Tel: 304-754-5077
http://www.nasw.org

This organization offers student memberships for those interested in opinion writing.
National Conference of Editorial Writers
3899 North Front Street
Harrisburg, PA 17110
Tel: 717-703-3015
Email: ncew@pa-news.org
http://www.ncew.org

For information about working as a writer and union membership, contact
National Writers Union
113 University Place, 6th Floor
New York, NY 10003
Tel: 212-254-0279
Email: nwu@nwu.org
http://www.nwu.org

This organization for journalists has campus and online chapters.
    Society of Professional Journalists (SPJ)
    Eugene S. Pulliam National Journalism Center
    3909 North Meridian Street
    Indianapolis, IN 46208
    Tel: 317-927-8000
    http://www.spj.org

For comprehensive information for citizens, students, and news people about the field of journalism, visit
    Project for Excellence in Journalism and the Committee of Concerned Journalists
    http://www.journalism.org

Index